WE NEED TO TALK

JONATHAN JANSEN

WE NEED TO TALK

MACMILLAN

BOOK**STORM**

© Jonathan Jansen 2011

Articles previously published as columns in *The Times*.

ISBN: 978-1-920434-16-8

First edition, first impression 2011

Published jointly by
Bookstorm (Pty) Limited and Pan Macmillan (Pty) Limited

PO Box 4532	Private Bag X19
Northcliff	Northlands
2115	2116
South Africa	South Africa

Distributed by Pan Macmillan
Via Booksite Afrika

Edited by Aïda Thorne
Proofread by Pat Botes
Cover design by Kevin Shenton
Author photograph by Stephen Collett
Typeset by Lebone Publishing Services
Printed and bound by Ultra Litho (Pty) Limited

ACKNOWLEDGMENTS

I happily acknowledge the source of all these stories, the thousands of people I have met across the length and breadth of this land. Your stories inspire me, and I hope to have done justice to the substance and spirit of our human encounters. To my unpaid critical reader of all these stories, my wife Grace, thank you. To my two beacons of decency, my children Mikhail and Sara-Jane, thank you for living lives of hope. A special word of thanks to *The Times* for allowing us to republish these stories in book form. A word of appreciation to Louise Grantham, one of the smartest publishers I have yet met. And to my distant friends in power, thank you for lousy governance; you give me something to write about.

ACKNOWLEDGMENTS

CONTENTS

TALK ABOUT UNIVERSITIES

TALK ABOUT LEADERSHIP

TALK ABOUT SOCIETY

TALK ABOUT SPORT AND THE 2010 WORLD CUP

EPILOGUE

INTRODUCTION

The rainbow in the rain

'I trace the rainbow in the rain and know the promise is not vain.' GEORGE MATHESON, 1882

The message on my Facebook page was heartrending: 'Professor Jansen, please say something to us people in Lindley to give us some hope, please.' I did not know the woman writing from this rural, eastern Free State town; it's what happens when you accept all the 'friend requests' that come your way on this social network facility called Facebook. But while the woman was a stranger, the context of her desperate appeal was not. Just the day before a gang of men had viciously murdered the Potgieter family and their little daughter Willemien.

Instead of a deep search for answers, such as 'How could this happen?', the punters fell back on convenience thinking – race. The problem with such convenience thinking is that an identical murder took place near Mariannhill around the same time: a black family burnt to death, with toddlers inside the flaming house, at the hands of fellow black South Africans. Clearly, the phenomenon of random and extreme violence calls for pause and reflection. How, indeed, could this happen so often, so intensely, so indiscriminately, so ubiquitously in our country? It requires, more than ever, that we talk about the rain and the rainbow, the pain and the hope.

For the past eighteen months I have done just that, travelling up and down the beloved country, talking to farmers, farm labourers, rural students, urban students, black and white citizens, rich and poor, old and young, Muslim and Jew, Christian and atheist, the angry and the contented ... in fact, talking to anyone who would listen, or who wanted to talk. While the immediate objectives of these visits were to represent the university; to rebuild its image in the broadest community; to win back the trust of alumni and to recruit future students, the longer-term objective was to understand this wonderful and wretched country and, on this basis, to contribute in a small way to its transformation after the cataclysm of apartheid.

I not only talked; I observed, watching how people respond to crises and how everyday life unfolds – from rural towns, where only the liquor store doubling as a butchery is the main source of economic activity in a town long deserted by the politicians, to a sophisticated company of JSE executives over dinner in classy chambers overlooking the most scenic night views of Johannesburg. I sat with primary school children on the ground in Douglas, and with the deputy president of the country in a university waiting room before we spoke. I watched how white people responded to my silly questions at the shop till: 'Do you have any discounts for black people?' And I examined closely the anxiety on the face of my black friend when she heard my daughter had a boyfriend: 'Is he black?'. When I hesitated (how on earth could his colour be important?), she followed up with a signifier: 'What is his name?'

Nothing is more revealing than talking to thousands of high school youth throughout the country. There is a liveliness there, an openness to the future, a desire for much more hopefulness about what kind of country this could be. Without exception, these young people are tired of hearing about the sins of the fathers (and mothers). They're shocked and despondent about what they see as the degradation of society by political youth, those thugs masked in party-political clothing and operating under cover of 'youth festivals', thus giving all young people a bad name. The energy, drive and optimism of these youth are what give impetus to so many of the stories recounted week after week in these columns reprinted from *The Times*.

What moved me most, however, were the ordinary South Africans living their lives well below the radar screen of mainstream media. These are the 'salt of the earth' people, hard-working citizens who eat their bread by the sweat of their collective brows. They are those single mothers abandoned by wayward men and who yet find the will and resources to put children through school. These are mothers who hold families together against unbelievable odds on the basis of a small set of core values – the virtues of hard work, the importance of respect, the necessity of discipline and the vitality of faith.

These mothers are seen in both townships and cities, and their offspring are easily recognised. Theirs are the children who wear the same clothes every day, but whose clothes are always clean with not a button missing, even though the buttons may not always match in colour or size.

These are the people who keep those thin threads called the 'fabric of society' together with little, if any, assistance from the bling-wielding nouveau riche that occupy newly found positions of status and power in government and business.

This does not mean that I am not intrigued by excess. Half-naked men and women slurping food from each other's bodies does raise questions about levels of depravity in one of the two most unequal countries on the planet. I find it incredible that the national lottery could give R40 million rand to a group of youngsters without the financial, organisational or social competence to run a spaza shop, and then wonder why this meeting of 'socialists' disintegrates into chaos.

It is so clear to me that 'public service' does not exist in our country and that, for most, being elected to a government position is a simple matter of personal enrichment and political egotism – it never was about service to the public. I spend a lot of time wondering how my former heroes who fought the struggle on an elevated platform of ethics and morality, putting their bodies and families on the line for our freedom, could participate in the most astounding decisions, such as denying access to the Dalai Lama, supporting the Aids policies of a president that led millions of the poorest among us to suffer and die needlessly, and vetoing votes in the United Nations against known tyrants from Burma to Zimbabwe. Where did our moral consciousness go?

The stories in this book will reveal my fascination with anger. Why are South Africans so angry? We not only protest, we also burn down and break down; we turn over garbage cans and beat each other senseless with chairs at political rallies; we threaten and, yes, we kill; we slander and we demean. Our soldiers, in anger, turn on the Union Buildings, the residence of their commander-in-chief. Where does this deep-seated anger come from? Why are we so prone to what appears to be spontaneous combustion? As I have argued through these columns, the anger comes from somewhere deep within ourselves and our history. This is something to be explained, for all around us there are poorer countries with more brutal colonial histories, but nothing compares with the anger and brutality of the citizens of the rainbow nation.

So, what is going on? There are at least three reasons for this extreme anger, violence and brutality in our society.

First, *we may be more traumatised than we think*. Because of the longevity and intensity of apartheid brutality, we did not recover. We were the last country in post-colonial Africa to taste freedom and democracy. The sheer duration of colonialism and apartheid over centuries stripped us of our dignity and so much of our humanity. Think back to grown men undressed under apartheid showers while their genitals were played with by the white police for the crime of not carrying a pass in the country of their birth. Think back to the systematic harassment of families night after night, year after year, decade after decade, and you begin to sense not only the duration, but also the intensity of the brutality. A Truth and Reconciliation Commission (TRC) was not going to undo this damage; what we need is a national trauma unit.

5

Second, *we internalised the brutality that we had to bear*. Burning people inside petrol-filled tyres is only possible when the perpetrator has lost his or her own humanity through earlier events. It is not only a response to the violence and violation of the human spirit; it is also the internalisation of that violence and violation. In the terms of that struggle, 'we became like them'. And that is why I have said over and over again that the only way out of this mess is together; yet the terms of engagement at the moment assume that the moral high ground belongs to the pure, unadulterated black victim laying material and symbolic claim and control over the impure, adulterated white perpetrator. That is a recipe for mutual annihilation of co-inhabitants of a common geographical space; of mutual burden-bearers of an intertwined trauma.

Third, *we did not mourn enough*. The Cypriot scholar and humanist, Michalinos Zembylas, talks about the necessity of victims of earlier conflicts, such as Greek and Turkish Cypriots, to mourn. Mourning the loss of the dead, which is so crucial to many cultures, especially African ones, is fundamental to both personal and societal recovery and transformation. We did not mourn, and where we did, it was not enough. We were rushed into a hurried TRC process in the hope that all would be revealed and we could start the process of mourning. But too many people still seek answers to the torture, murders and disappearances. We forced closure before those who suffered were ready for it. We urged ordinary people into rainbow thinking when all they could see was the rain.

There is only one way out of this moral and political quagmire. We must talk. In churches, mosques, temples and synagogues; in schools and universities; in government and in civil society; in families and sports clubs; on buses, in taxis and on trains. We must talk about our troubles. Too many South Africans murmur the words of that Negro spiritual: 'Nobody knows the troubles I've seen.' That's the problem; nobody knows.

This was the raison d'être for the column in *The Times*. It was to prise open hearts and minds, and for this the strategy was simple. 'What,' asked a friend, 'is the key to being a successful columnist?' I proposed two rules. Rule #1: Always upset 50 per cent of your reading audience. Rule #2: Make sure it's not the same 50 per cent as the previous week. One of the pedagogical techniques used for this purpose is to pose complex dilemmas for discussion. The dilemmas should be provocative enough to draw out immediate responses, but subtle enough to require thought. Take, for example, a recent entry on my Facebook status page, the aim of which is to draw my several hundred (mainly) student friends into engaging in tough political dilemmas. Here it is:

I have just returned from a disturbing visit to the National War Museum in Bloemfontein, formerly the Anglo-Boer War Museum. I looked into the haunting eyes of a 16-year-old Afrikaner boy called Johannes Petrus Coetzee who was executed by the English in 1901 for resistance to the Imperialist invasion. Here's my question: should he be afforded the same status in history as Solomon Mahlangu?

And yet, for productive and hopeful talking to take place, a number of things first have to be in place.

To begin with, we need to *recognise our mutual pain*. As long as the historical narrative retains 'good black victims' versus 'bad white perpetrators', we don't stand a chance of reconstructing and reconciling in the beloved country. I see, feel and fear daily the relentless one-line, anti-white narrative in circles in which I move and, disturbingly, among young black South Africans. This is bad news over the long term, unless we change the story about the past and the vision about the future. We must tell our children that the perpetrators of apartheid were black and white, and that stories of interracial solidarity were as much a reality in the struggle against apartheid as the brute oppression by a white minority government. And that history is more complex and messed up than we tell our inheritors, and that it must change.

Black anger and the thirst for vengeance must be dealt with. In this regard, we must recognise an important phenomenon – the race card. I have noticed that the wolf-cry of racism often has nothing to do with race or racial affrontation. More often than not, the immediate reasons for the invocation of race has to do with other things, like incompetence, poverty, general hardship, feeling stuck in one's dire circumstances, and sheer laziness. Then, and for all these reasons, a culprit must be found. Nothing is more convenient and more devastating (for the one charged) than the accusation of racism against a historical enemy.

We must also *deal with the knowledge streams that filter messages* about the past and the future into the minds of our young people. Places of learning, both formal and non-formal, must be charged with telling the stories of both despair and hope, of oppression and freedom, of reconciliation and social justice, of struggle and responsibility, of fairness and forgiveness, of ethnic nationalism and non-racial solidarity. These twin themes of history must be interwoven in the way we tell our stories. Narratives of bitterness and retaliation that reboot the human memory to restore the tired storyline of white enemies and black victims are dangerous. This storyline labels black people who refuse to fall into this narrative trap with vicious tags, such as 'coconuts', 'counter-revolutionaries' and (believe it or not) racists. It is a tactic designed to intimidate and humiliate those who step out of the prescribed lines of the old racial narrative.

We must then *deal with political language*; those messages that come from powerful citizens, and that shape in powerful ways the attitudes and behaviours of ordinary citizens. In poor countries with large numbers of illiterate citizens, a special responsibility rests on those in political power to be vigilant and careful when using racial language. One success story that illustrates this point was when the government with one voice and with consistent language spoke out against xenophobia. Slowly, the tension eased.

One catastrophic story of failure was when the government deliberately sent mixed messages about HIV/Aids and the efficacy of drug treatments, with tens of thousands marching to their graves. What the president, his cabinet and all political office-bearers at the three levels of government say makes a huge difference on the ground. Take a hypothetical case: a Minister of Agriculture who dismisses the deaths of white farmers and their families on farms or smallholdings with contemptuous statements, such as 'Black people are also murdered daily', does much more harm to race relations than an undiluted, compassionate response to both situations.

When a sitting president continues to sing 'Bring me my machine gun', it might indeed hold wonderful struggle remembrances for political blacks. But it is, quite frankly, provocative this side of democracy. It breeds racial distrust and suspicion, and it lays the groundwork for racial retaliation when the economic or political chips are down. It ignores the fact that black people now hold power. This is the danger of not thinking long term; of presuming innocence in the words we use; of being one-sided in our celebration of history and our perspective on society.

We urgently have to *deal with the underlying distress among the poor*, especially the education system. The longer the school system fails hundreds of thousands of Grade 12 learners every year, the more inevitable becomes the resurgence of race identities and race thinking among black South Africans. As I have regularly argued, young people do not just drop out, they drop into lives of desperation, poverty, anger, hatred, crime and violence. Those layers of angry youth have been piling up steadily before and since 1994. I hate this metaphor, but we are definitely sitting on a time bomb. **I warn all South Africans: there is racial trouble ahead if we do not solve the crisis of having two school systems in a sea of inequality** – a small, elite, well-functioning system for the black and white middle classes, and a massive, dysfunctional, impoverished system for the majority of poor black children.

We must open up channels allowing us to *deal effectively with the wrongdoings of the past*. There is too much trauma underlying the tragedy of a violent and angry citizenry. Tens of thousands of middle-aged white men suffer daily the double tragedy of having done terrible things during the war inside the country, on its borders and through 'incursions' into the region; and of having no release valve for their anger, confusion and bitterness. There is a dangerous post-traumatic stress present that I witnessed during 2010 as I spoke at men's conferences around the country.

It is no accident that the fastest-growing genre of new books in South Africa is by men writing about the border wars. Fascinatingly, these books fall into two broad categories – those who defend their actions as heroic victors over the 'communist agitators', and those who decry the senseless battles defending the indefensible. Both responses reflect traumatic categories – the one being unable, or unwilling, to come to terms with an unbearable truth; the other seeking respite from the powerful who sent them to war for nothing. It is a great pity that the non-Afrikaans-speaking citizenry did not have access to the so-called Boetman series of writing by Chris Louw taking issue with De Klerk and the powerful on behalf of white apartheid youth for their sacrifices during the war, all brought to a meaningless end with the recognition that they were in fact shoring up an *evil regime* (my words).

The more obvious trauma, however, is that of millions of black South Africans who were bypassed during, or missed out on, or did not qualify for participation in the TRC hearings. I know this might hurt some of my white brothers and sisters, but I often get the impression in the areas where I have worked that many people do not have a clue about the depth of hurt and the scale of tragedy that apartheid wrought on ordinary black South Africans. There is a minority that still thinks apartheid was not all that bad, being simply a matter of separate arrangements for white and black and, after all, 'black people should be grateful for civilisation'. This is powder keg stuff; a recipe for racial conflagration; an idiocy that is hard to fathom.

It was, of course, not only the structural dimensions of apartheid, the systematic dispossession of property and lives that mattered, and which explains the huge racialised inequalities of today. It was the daily rituals of humiliation and distress, captured so poignantly in Leon Wessels' retelling of a disturbing incident in Mark Mathabane's award-winning book, *Kaffir Boy*.*

Mark tells how his father aged before his eyes when the police dragged him naked from under the bed during a passbook inspection in a white area. While the policeman asked his father questions about his passbook, the officer played around with the older man's private parts

* Retold on p. 311 of *Vereeniging, die onvoltooide vrede*, by Leon Wessels, 2010, Umuzi, Random House Struik. Originally published in *Why race matters in South Africa*, by Michael MacDonald. (Translated from Afrikaans by the author.)

with his police baton, much to the amusement of the other policemen in the room. The son's mother was spared this humiliation, as she was not discovered hiding in the small clothing cupboard in her underwear.

It is the memory of such multiplied traumas over decades and centuries, handed down from one generation to the next through, what I once called, 'knowledge in the blood', which is still not dealt with and which poisons race and human relations today.

How do we work our way through these traumas of white and black South Africans? The worst thing we can do is pretend they do not exist and hope that time will heal and sort out traumatic memories. Big mistake. They will come back to hurt us, not always in the explosive confrontations of black versus white, as seen at Ventersdorp, nor always in the dreadful, unresolved pain taken to the grave, but in everyday relationships of hurt, guilt, bitterness and resentment. These chip away at human relations in schools, universities, factory floors, mining companies, manufacturing plants, religious practices, domestic relations and everyday social shavings between white and black on streets, beaches, shops and public transport.

We know that direct confrontation does not work. We know that accusatory finger-pointing is unproductive. We know that one-off performances of truth and reconciliation are not durable. We know that provoking guilt and shame scares the other side into silence or retaliation. The Reitz decision offers a possible model of how to proceed.

The 'what' of the Reitz decision has enjoyed extensive coverage on both sides of human judgment. What has been less well covered was the 'why' of the decision to not pursue institutional charges against the four former students, and to invite them back to complete their studies. Why? For three reasons:

First, in order to deal with institutional racism it was not enough to single out the four perpetrators of a racist deed. They could be thrown into prison, so to speak, and institutional racism would continue. What was important was that individual culpability, as well as institutional complicity, be dealt with in the calculation of what went wrong when four young white men decided to make a statement against a mild anti-integration policy in the university residences by pretending to urinate into a concoction given to five senior black workers to imbibe. The decision by the institution to ask forgiveness of black (and white) people for what had happened, was a statement of owning up to the university's historic role in shaping and sustaining the racist attitudes of white youth.

Second, in order to deal with the individual racism of the four students the institution, as a place of higher learning, had an educative responsibility for bringing the students back into education in order to engage them on their attitudes, ideas and behaviour towards other people. Putting four young men out to pasture without the capabilities to confront their racial ghosts made them a danger to all of society and, importantly, to themselves. The courts would deal with the criminal and civil cases against the former students. The five workers would have to decide when and whether to forgive and reconcile with the four students whom they knew well and trusted. The institution, however, was an agent in this matter and had to take a position – which it did.

Third, in order to deal with the thirst for revenge and retaliation, the institution desired to set a higher example of what was possible when the language of condemnation was replaced with language of conciliation; when justice was accompanied by grace; and retaliation was displaced by restoration. There are far too many examples of such acts of reconciliation in the country, by great and small, to pretend that this was something unique. It was a decision that recognised the limits of legal reasoning in resolving deep-seated human problems. It was a decision that consciously countered the hubris of the powerful as it sought to extract a price on the heads of these young men and, figuratively speaking, hang them in the public square.

The effects of this decision went beyond our expectations. Within days there was a groundswell of support from across South Africa and other countries lauding the path we had chosen. Across the racial divide, streams of correspondence and calls hailed the decision; people who had left the country promised to come back, given a sense that this was, after all, a place for their children too.

Within the campus community, ground was suddenly opened up to advance deep transformation in ways that would have been much more difficult outside the politics of grace and accommodation. The data showed an immediate positive swing, with 40 per cent more students reporting positive race relations than in the period before the Reitz decision. Top black and white academics applied, and many were accepted, to join a university which they saw as opening up new possibilities for scholarship in public.

At all levels of the organisation the team worked day and night to create a new institutional culture among students and staff. Academic (and not race-obsessive) contests took centre stage, and compulsory class attendance and increased admission requirements were implemented. A new core curriculum was introduced to provide an intellectual basis for the education of young people, in which they were challenged to take on the big questions of life from the vantage point of science, religion, astronomy and economics. Questions of race, identity and change featured prominently in this interdisciplinary core. Everybody reported a much more positive atmosphere and a consistently inclusive approach to transformation.

Of course, this kind of transformation threatened loud voices in a divided society. It threatened the powerful, those in government, who saw reconciliation as the proprietary right of the ruling party. Not surprisingly, soon after the university's decision, the media reported an attempt by the powerful to release the apartheid killer Eugene de Kock as a gesture of reconciliation. However, neither white nor black supported this move at all and the plan backfired. Next, a trip was scheduled to Orania and Verwoerd's wife, another gesture of the accommodation of white separatists who had cordoned off a strip of barren land for white occupation in the Northern Cape. The presidency suddenly discovered poor whites again.

This explains the fiery outbursts from the powerful. I became the first vice-chancellor of a university in the history of South Africa to be roundly condemned by the cabinet for an institutional decision, and the first to be attacked in public by both the Minister and his political Director-General (DG) in waves of personal attack, in the media and in private circles, as it came to my attention.

Reconciliation of this kind also threatened some segments of the white Afrikaner community. One Chris Louw launched a scathing attack: 'Come off your cross', he screamed – the symbolism of care and forgiveness stretching across racial lines and against the logic of racial expectations was too much for the brilliant thinker to bear. Weeks later the troubled man ended his life. Among some Afrikaner intellectuals the critique was stiff, especially in the light of my book, *Knowledge in Blood*, which carries the theme of mutual destiny, mutual vulnerability and mutual recognition.

What was disconcerting to such a group was the return of the anthropological gaze, a black man studying the once-powerful, thereby upsetting the accepted order of scholarly inquiry that had prevailed for hundreds of years. One leader of a conservative Afrikaner youth group admonished his followers not to take me seriously: 'Jansen is coloured' – a term I always detested and assign no meaning to – 'and knows nothing about us Afrikaners.'

There were others who made sustained personal attacks and remained hell-bent on tainting the institution as racist for as long as possible – all other institutions, of course, were stainless, especially the English ones. One such source was the *Sunday Independent*, which relentlessly pursued dirt on the institution and its leadership, often running besmirching personal attacks that became more and more childish with time. The screaming headlines (labelling me a coconut) bore no relationship even to the manufactured content of their stories.

The real test of the Reitz decision, of course, was whether it would make possible the grounds for genuine reconciliation between the workers and the former students. On 25 February 2011, the culmination of years of hard work by an incredible team from the university and the provincial leader of the Human Rights Commission bore fruit in the final reconciliation ceremony (this while the rest of the HRC at the Johannesburg offices behaved more and more like the ruling party in legal drag). The students prepared their hearts to ask for forgiveness; the workers were ready to accept the plea and to offer that grace which lifts both the one who asks and the one who gives. Tears flowed freely and hearts were mended.

By this time, of course, the Reitz event had taken on national and even international meanings for divided communities and campuses everywhere. Universities in other countries asked the University of the Free State (UFS) to facilitate reconciliation deliberations on their campuses. Churches and community groups in South Africa filled the diary requesting workshops and speeches that would open up their own settings to difficult dialogues about race and reconciliation, healing and hope.

We had come through the storm; the rainbow shone brightly and the rain was gone.

The question often asked about Reitz (I use the noun here to refer to the racist incident, as well as the entire swath of decisions and actions related to Reitz afterwards, including the acts of forgiveness) is how we knew that this was the correct decision. Surely, the risks were self-evident?

I have made some mistakes in my life, but this is not one of them. As soon as the decision on institutional forgiveness hit the media, a call came through from the political DG: 'I might disagree with your decision, but I know you would have thought about it carefully.' Her attitude changed quickly after that, as the political climate cancelled out reasonableness and tamed the quest for understanding. Indeed, the decision was carefully thought through and planned months in advance, and in conversation with all major stakeholders.

A careful assessment of what I saw and heard, and a fine understanding of how the institution (as at the University of Pretoria) was shaping the lives and reinforcing the behaviours of young white Afrikaner men, enabled the decision. But it was the overwhelming sense – before the announcement – of what such an act of institutional forgiveness would do for campus and country that had firmed the resolve we would embrace.

In the ruling party, all hell broke loose, but with an ominous silence (unnoticed at the time) from one group in the ascendancy after Polokwane – that landmark conference of the African National Congress that removed a sitting president from office – the ANC Youth League. There was therefore an instant adrenalin rush in the media when the League promptly announced that it planned to visit me at 10:00 on an appointed day.

That day I arrived at work earlier than usual and the cameras were already out in front of my office. There was an atmosphere of 'High Noon on Red Square', that curiously named patch of reddish brick pavement that stretches across the front of the main building, and on which the statue of the president of the Orange Free State republic stands tall. The crowd built up steadily for the showdown. A few minutes after 10:00 my cellphone rang: 'Prof., I'll be a few minutes late.'

What happened next can be interpreted from two main vantage points, and more about that in a minute.

Mr Julius Malema showed up with a posse of not-too-young black men, looking drawn and serious. The two delegations sat down in the large room next to my office. I had decided at the last minute to bring a delegation of my own, because this time I wanted witnesses to what was discussed – the lies and denials from previous meetings with important people had made me more cautious about showing up alone. The two delegations eyed each other.

I welcomed the visitors and told them about my respect for the ANC Youth League as a historical formation, and the great honour that I had had at Cornell University of being taught by one of its founding members, the great humanitarian and Professor of Africana Studies, Comrade Mbata. It was because of the historical and political significance of the League that I felt honoured to welcome the current leadership. 'Over to you, Mr Malema.'

I had given this short history lesson before, when Mr Malema came to the Mangosuthu University of Technology, where I was administrator ('rescuer-in-chief' when a university falls apart) at the time of the elections. The university climate was on a knife-edge, as ancient hostilities between students supporting the Inkatha Freedom Party (Sadesmo) and those supporting the ANC (Sasco) were literally at each other's throats. That was when I first saw the capacity of the man, Malema, to manage a large-scale crisis and contain what would otherwise have been a bloody start to the national and provincial elections of 2009.

He started to speak, and by now the singing and chanting of the crowds outside my office windows pointed to a potentially explosive event. 'Maybe Prof. can explain why he did what he did.' Of course, the reference was to the decision to forgive institutional charges against the Reitz Four and invite those with incomplete degrees to come back and complete their studies.

I sketched the context for the decision, the institutional complicity in producing students with racist attitudes and beliefs, and the failure to act against racism embedded in the organisation of separate classes, separate residences and separate social spaces everywhere. I also pointed out that restoration of the social and academic mandate of the university required leading two groups, one white and one black, and that a few strategic decisions – like the one to forgive – would open up the space for fundamental transformation of the UFS, which would not be possible if the hardened lines of division and retaliation continued to exist as in the current climate. That speech took about 40 minutes.

Halfway through the impromptu speech I literally saw
the change of expression on Mr Malema's face. One or two
of my colleagues sensed this as well, and I saw glistening
eyes among them. Something had changed even before
the leader of the Youth League could respond.

'Prof., they always present you as a hard man in the
media, but you are reasonable in the way you say things.' A
Youth League leader did not like this meeting of the minds
and attempted to drag us back into anger. 'The Prof. has
spoken,' said Mr Malema with a firm voice and the chal-
lenger backed down.

Mr Malema agreed with the decision. He insisted that
students had to be brought back into learning and not
kept away from their studies – and this included the young
men from Reitz. He wanted them to come back in ways
that empowered the former students to confront what
they did wrong, and that enabled the broader university
community to participate in a TRC-type event where experiences of racism and alienation could be expressed and
dealt with. He felt sure that the five workers in the case
would be open to such a resolution of the matter, and that
the whole institution would benefit from such a process of
restoration.

For a few minutes, the people in the room drifted
around each other in disbelief. There was one problem,
though – the crowd outside (many of whom were not
from the university) was baying for blood and the media
never had it so good. I harboured some doubts – would
Mr Malema actually convey the spirit and substance of

that meeting to the crowd? Would he deliver his bold plan for reconciliation to his constituency?

Since the Red Square is adjacent to my office, the build-up of noise was intense. My shutters were drawn so that the crowd could not see into my working space and become even more agitated. It was now a matter of waiting. Suddenly, everything went quiet. I heard two or three sharp announcements; then some deep groans. Then quiet. I lifted the shutters – there was no one on the square. My cellphone rang; it was Mr Malema. 'Prof., it was tough, but we did the right thing. I am now leaving campus.' My emotions got the better of me.

What had happened? How does one explain this unexpected turn of events?

To the community of faith, the positive conclusion to the meeting between Jansen and Malema was a matter of spiritual intervention. My secretary reminds me of the rural farmer who called early that High Noon morning to say he had prayed through the night, and that I should not prepare for the meeting but that the words would be given me to speak at the right time. It was at this point that my telephone and email systems started to record similar messages: people from different faiths had stayed up to pray in the days leading to the meeting. Many church leaders spoke about all-night prayer vigils. This was truly astounding, with total strangers in prayer all over the country. This was a deeply, deeply humbling experience for me, and as I moved across the country, the stories of solidarity in prayer were heard over and over again.

To the political rationalist, the positive conclusion was further evidence of the influence and independence of the Youth League leader in making important decisions outside of his party's viewpoint. This action had retained him at the forefront of national politics shortly after he co-led the movement to bring down the previous president, Thabo Mbeki. Others saw him making up lost ground for the ANC, with the party and the cabinet already having condemned the decision and the principle. The Youth League leader had placed the ANC back in the reconciliation business, as evidence emerged of broad public support for the decision, including the voice of the Nobel Laureate Desmond Tutu.

I am not sure Mr Malema's team liked the media response, for it mischievously presented the outcome as being the influence of a senior teacher on a younger learner, the 'taming' of a fierce and forceful youth leader, the result of 'going to school' and being taught well. This was unfortunate, for the Youth League leader is, in fact, a strong leader with significant influence over the future direction of politics in South Africa. Such an evaluation is not to condone the behaviour or decisions of Malema or his League; it is a simple, objective assessment based on a close-up observation of his leadership away from the crowds.

Which brings us back to the present, and the underlying reasons for the newspaper columns represented in this collection, and future writings and musings on the no-longer-new South Africa. We are entering a development period of smokes and mirrors in our democracy. The public now knows that political promises about more jobs and houses, or better health and education, are not going to happen. The public knows that the only way to get the attention of the powerful is to engage in violent protests that make it into the news. The public knows that the big men are there to eat, and that radical rhetoric about a socialist future is nothing but a cover for party greed and personal advancement.

Enter the magicians.

There was a Blatterish-feel to the moment in January 2011 when the Minister of Basic Education lifted a huge cardboard to reveal to the media the national Grade 12 pass rate for public schools. The pass rate had jumped by more than 7 per cent over that of the previous year. 'Too good to be true', railed one national newspaper; 'out with the truth', demanded another. The media had seen this movie before during the years of Education Minister Kader Asmal, when national pass marks in matric shot up by double digits, only to drop to depressing lows again when it became clear that there must have been massive manipulation of raw scores to get tens of thousands more students passing in less than twelve months.

The economic chips are down, however. People are being laid off. Houses fall apart. Trash is not collected. Sewage runs in streets. Potholes accumulate. Fuel prices rise. Toilets have no enclosures. Children get meaningless school certificates that do not enable them to find jobs or enter higher education. To make matters worse, there are national and municipal elections coming up, and the small elite that benefits from these convulsive episodes called 'elections' needs the poor to keep them in power.

There is no better playground for obfuscatory politics than these Grade 12 results. How do those in power do it? First, you look at the actual raw scores of more than 600 000 students and you panic. You see that more than half of these young people tend to fail, and this will be a political disaster in the year before national elections. Second, you pretend that you have an independent body that authorises the results without any political scrutiny whatsoever. Third, you allow that body to raise the marks for no less than nineteen subjects so that tens of thousands more pass than would have been the case if the raw scores had been accepted. Fourth, you tell the public that such statistical moderation is completely normal, but too complex for them to understand – for that reason, your independent body will not reveal how and why the statistical adjustments were made to enable these massive leaps in the national pass rate. Fifth, you call anyone who dares to ask questions about these examination results 'counter-revolutionaries' or 'racists' and hope the problem goes away.

No magician tells you how that dove popped out of his hat, or why the woman was not actually sawn in half, as you think you saw. If that happens, he is out of a job. And so the audience of adults plays along, for there is no harm done to the young children that you brought along for the game of smoke and mirrors. The difference between the magician and the politician is that the magician knows that what he does is harmless and not true.

In conclusion

I have written these columns to try and strip away political pretence, and to offer another view on what passes as 'good for you', like old, dead chickens injected with refresher chemicals for resale to the poor to buy and eat. I write because I am deeply committed to our democracy and know that the day we begin to embrace self-censorship out of fear or favour is the day we begin to dig the political grave of the rainbow nation. I write because there are stories to be told of hope and healing spread across this land, in the lives of extraordinary people without whom we would have no country to speak of. But, mostly, I write because I know of no greater joy than to express in words the promise of that rainbow that lies behind the rain.

TALK ABOUT SCHOOLS

*'The dilemma we face, of course,
is that yet another generation of youth
would have seen twelve years
of poor and inconsistent teaching.'*

Impossible without a dramatic intervention

Grade 12 results, 2010

13 January 2011

The first reaction was one of pure delirium. The second reaction was deeply troubling. 'Out with the truth,' screamed the headline on the front page of an Afrikaans Sunday newspaper. 'Too good to be true,' was the lead article on the front page of a new English daily. If the senior certificate results were so good, why would consternation reign among the thinking public? Why would a civic forum take legal steps requiring the body that assures the quality of the Grade 12 examinations to explain the sharp increase in pass rates? It's quite simple, really: we had seen this happen before, during the years when Kader Asmal was Minister of Education and when, to the horror of 'matric watchers', the results spiked from 48.9 per cent in 1999 to 73.3 per cent in 2003!

The reason thinking people are sceptical is because, within a period of twelve months, about 7 per cent more learners passed Grade 12 than in the previous year. Remember, we are talking about very large numbers of candidates. This means that many thousands of students must have passed at a much higher rate than the previous year for this pass rate to have been achieved.

In a small school with, say, 200 senior certificate candidates, a 7 per cent growth in the pass rate would raise some eyebrows, but would be considered within the bounds of possibility, given the modest student numbers. In a system where close to 538 000 students write the examination, 7 per cent growth is impossible **unless** there has been dramatic intervention during a twelve-month period that could explain the magnitude of the pass rate.

The problem for the Department of Basic Education is that there has been no dramatic intervention on the scale required. In fact, there were major disruptions due to the Soccer World Cup, the protracted strike by public servants (which included mainly teachers from disadvantaged schools) and, of course, the time routinely lost in township schools every year as a matter of bad habit.

The reasons proffered by oversensitive officials so far are disingenuous. Politicians and public servants – increasingly the same people – have claimed in recent days that the reasons for the spike included the fact that 'the Minister visited schools', or 'the media encouraged students to learn', or 'everybody pulled their weight', or 'after the strike, students and teachers got serious about examination preparation'. In my business there is something called evidence, and these reasons constitute speculative bluff and nonsense reasoning. If, indeed, as many claim, the massively positive response from the public after the teachers' strike explains the positive results, then my policy recommendation would be that we organise a three-week strike every year just before the Grade 12 examinations – and, before you know it, there would be another spike in the results.

These results are not a real reflection of positive knowledge gains among Grade 12 learners, and every honest public official knows that. That is the simple reason why Umalusi refuses to make public the processes by which adjustments were made to no less than nineteen subjects in the 2010 examination. They refuse, because to reveal that process – in other words, being accountable to the public for a public examination – will cause major political embarrassment to the government.

Unfortunately, our journalists are generally very tame and often intimidated by bullying officials. They should, however, ask Umalusi questions such as the following:

- What would the pass rate have been if the raw scores had been accepted for all the written subjects, and not only for some of them?
- Why exactly were the adjustments made for the specific subjects, and by what margin and for what reasons?
- What were the early interactions between the government and Umalusi in discussions of the initial results, and what were the decisions made about the adjustments in the end?

The government statisticians often sell a sad story when confronted with these kinds of questions. They argue that statistical moderation of raw test or exam results is normal in any large education system because it is unlikely that intelligence or performance can change dramatically within one year. True. What they do not tell you is that the claim is only valid **within a stable system**. And the last thing South Africa can lay claim to is that we have, or have had, a stable system, especially in 2010.

Until the government and its quality assurance agency can convince the public once and for all that the statistical moderation of examination scores is not, in fact, the political moderation of unacceptable examination data, the public will remain sceptical, and for good reason.

Zim can teach us a thing or two

The country's schools work; its teachers really teach

2 December 2010

When faced with the choice between two teachers, one from Zimbabwe and one from South Africa, I would choose the Zimbabwean one without any further question.

It is not simply because the Zimbabwean teacher is likely to know more mathematics or physical science than the average South African teacher. It's about the crucial fact that the Zimbabwean teacher is likely to work much harder than the native South African.

The Zimbabwean educator is not the kind of teacher who is likely to demand more sick leave even before she gets ill. She is not used to taking off the last payday of the month to do her banking and shopping. She is certainly not one to give up weeks of teaching time to further her own salary interests. The Zimbabwean teacher, despite a low salary and poor working conditions, is at heart a professional who places the child at the centre of her duty.

I was one of those optimistic South Africans who made my way to Zimbabwe in the late 1980s to study its highly successful school system. Despite the fact that the war had destroyed many rural schools, there was something in the culture and character of Zimbabwean schools that drove their success.

Like many activists, I too sneered at the Cambridge examination syndicate on which its curriculum and examinations were based, considering it a nasty relic of British colonialism. I mean, how could a proclaimed socialist state (which, of course, Zimbabwe never was) cling so uncritically to the educational instruments of its own oppressors?

I now temper that criticism with a good dose of pragmatism, for the Zimbabweans did not throw out the education baby with the ideological bathwater – they kept in place what was working. If only the 'gods' of outcomes-based education had learnt from education reforms across the border.

Of course, I am generalising. There are many good South African teachers on both sides of the resource divide, who struggle against the odds not to succumb to the rising tide of mediocrity in the public school system. To those teachers I doff my hat. My problem is with the majority, the close to 80 per cent of teachers who will not blink an eyelid when a few hundred thousand children again fail the senior certificate examinations.

The dilemma we face, of course, is that yet another generation of youth would have seen twelve years of poor and inconsistent teaching, and pull up their noses at the noble profession. And so the cycle of despair continues, and worsens.

Ask yourself: what were the dominant images of schools in the press in recent months? In other words, what picture of schools, teachers and students did observant teenagers in school have of these important public institutions?

They would have read, heard and seen on television endless images of a school called Jules High. They would have seen pictures of sex on the playgrounds; rumours of rape and date-rape drugs being available; teachers laughing at the spectacle (whether true or not) and – heaven forbid – they would have seen the mobile phone images of child sex circulating among friends. That was the second half of the year.

During the middle of the year, they would have experienced long stay-aways from school, boredom at home, idleness on the streets and teachers who simply didn't care a damn while hours upon hours of instructional time were lost.

At the beginning of the year, they would have observed the weeks whittling away while schools tried to admit students, finalise timetables and basically wait for the spirit of the summer vacation to wear off.

If I were a desperate township parent who could not get my child into a fancy school in a suburb, I would take the risk of being an illegal immigrant and flee across the border in the opposite direction – into Zimbabwe. Yes, they do have a tyrant for a president and sometimes they lack bread in the shops, but at least the schools work and the teachers teach.

Instead of protesting about service delivery that might never come, I would campaign for thousands of Zim teachers to be given special professional visas by Home Affairs and special housing by Human Settlements. I would do anything to get my child educated, for this is the one thing that can break the cycle of domestic poverty: my child in the hands of a dedicated, knowledgeable, professional teacher.

Can you blame such a parent?

Matric exams not 'do or die'

Senior certificate results don't determine a learner's future

27 October 2010

Dear Matriculant Class of 2010

I'm sure that by now you are tired of hearing all the advice about your senior certificate examinations, and about how the Grade 12 results will determine your future. Your teachers and parents must be at you all the time about putting in every effort, for 'this is it!'

Actually, much of what you have heard in the run-up to the examinations is very bad advice.

First of all, the Grade 12 examinations do not determine your future. In fact, most universities no longer look at the Grade 12 results alone, but also at a range of other assessments, including the national benchmark tests, to determine whether to admit you to higher learning or not. Some university programmes might even interview you in order to get beyond the paperwork and see whether you have what it takes to succeed at university and in the world of work.

You see, what they do not tell you, is that many universities do not trust the senior certificate results, even though the standard of the examinations is much more credible than it was about ten years ago.

Second, as you know, it is possible in South Africa to pass some subjects with a 30 or 40 per cent mark. If this is your aim, my advice to you is to spare yourself the pressure of the final examinations. Go to a beach somewhere and sell seaweed to fishermen, for your prospects at university or in society are completely non-existent if you take the standards of the Department of Basic Education as your passing goal.

So, go into that examination with the aim of passing well. Our school system is based on mediocrity, not excellence; it bestows favour on those who scrape through, rather than those who outstrip their potential. A pass of 30 per cent means that you are clueless about 70 per cent of the work. Show some self-respect and aim for the top of your class!

Third, there is little you can do in the last month before an examination. Adults have lied to you if they have pushed you into cram schools or spring camps under the illusion that you can take three years of senior learning and squeeze this into your head within a few weeks. All that nonsense you hear about students studying all night and then writing the examination the next morning is extremely dangerous.

The month before and the night before are a time to rest; to do simple revision and not to stress yourself. The brain, unlike other muscles, is a sophisticated organ – not one that can be subjected to sudden press-ups just before a race.

Fourth, and this is going to hurt, but if you did not study steadily all year round, you are not going to pass. If you did not use the time productively while your teachers went on that prolonged and destructive strike, expect the worst. I know this is a terrible thing to say, but it is much better for you to hear the truth now and prepare yourself for the outcome, than to raise your hopes and have them dashed later.

I know of a lazy, but earnest evangelical student who sat for his matric physics exam many years ago and prayed as he lifted the pen to write: 'Speak Lord, Your servant heareth.' Needless to say, his physical science results were rotten.

Fifth, and this is going to hurt even more, at least two of your subjects have nothing to do with your further education. The one is life orientation and the other is mathematical literacy. Don't get me wrong; any meaningful learning in these two areas will probably make you a better citizen or a more informed consumer – stuff like that. Do not for one moment, however, think that mathematical literacy will boost your chances of higher education; even weaker universities now realise that a good mark in math lit is a poor predictor of success.

Sixth, most of you should not go to university to begin with. Society has given you the wrong message about post-school learning opportunities. I hope more and more of you will pursue high-quality vocational training through further education and training (FET) colleges or their equivalent. Much is being done to ensure that these colleges improve the three critical things needed for quality vocational training: highly skilled personnel, top-quality equipment, and a positive teaching and learning climate.

Seventh, you are smarter than any examination can foretell. If you do well, congratulations. If not, one page of poor results is not the end of the world. I'll be holding thumbs for all of you. Write well.

How to start fixing our schools

Take politics out of basic education; replace with panel of experts

20 October 2010

Dear President Zuma

I am writing to you out of desperation.

Desperation is an emotion I seldom feel, except in relation to education, for I believe very deeply that for most of our children, a solid school education represents the only means available for ending the cycle of family poverty. Skills come later; economic growth even later. Social cohesion lies far in the distance. What matters is that children complete twelve years of schooling with the ability to read, write, reason, calculate and express confidence for the purposes of further studies, skills training and higher education.

At various moments during your leadership, I have been encouraged, sir, by your standpoint on education. You are absolutely correct in insisting on teachers being in school, teaching every day. You are right, of course, to insist on materials being available for learning. You cannot be faulted for requiring performance contracts from the Ministers who report to you on progress in education. Your own biography as a man who has sacrificed his own schooling in the broader quest for liberation is something I admire.

The problem, Mr President, is the distance existing between what you stand for, and the day-to-day operations of schools in our country.

Unlike most of your MECs for education, I do not for one moment believe the crisis in schooling lies within the schools themselves. Having visited thousands of schools over the past decades, and having spoken to (and taught) thousands of pupils across the nine provinces, I can assure you that the children are the least of your problems.

With the right leadership and authority in place, with enthusiastic teachers ready to teach, and with organisational routines (like starting on time, doing homework every day, giving solid teaching, and so on) running like clockwork, children anywhere in the world respond positively to the efforts of adults to educate them. So, I am not speaking about the children.

It is clear to me that, at the moment, the control of schools does not rest with the government. It rests with the teachers' unions. Until this simple fact is acknowledged, it is impossible to create the kinds of conditions in and around schooling that provide for predictable teaching timetables and powerful learning environments.

This, I know, is difficult terrain for public discussion. After all, the largest teachers' union is part of the massive labour federation, which plays a critical role in who stays in, or comes to, power in the next rounds of election.

But, Mr President, I believe you can, and should, look beyond the politics of succession that comes in five-year cycles, and look to the long-term development of the country and the prospects of tens of thousands of young people who routinely fail examinations every year and who fuel the numbers of frustrated youth that turn on society and themselves. This is the single most important challenge you are facing and it cannot be resolved by pedagogical means, only through political intervention.

To signal your seriousness about this crisis, sir, I propose you appoint an 'Education Crisis Panel of Experts' to guide you and our government on how to resolve the education standoff as a matter of urgency. Please do not appoint activists to this panel, unless they are also experts; and do not see these appointments as ways of rewarding loyalty in the past or present – there are other commissions that can, and have, achieved such objectives.

Ensure, Mr President, that these are people who actually know how to turn schools around and who are unlikely to tell you what you want to hear. You made an excellent start by hiring Dr Cassius Lubisi as your Director-General. I have worked with him for many years; you will not find a person of greater integrity, passion and insight. Perhaps he could chair the panel.

I propose, if I may, the following names: Linda Vilikazi-Tselane, Muavia Gallie, Anita Maritz, James Letuka, Brian Isaacs, Sibusiso Maseko, Nontsha Liwane-Mazengwe, Stephen Lowry, Sharon Lewin, Itumeleng Molale and Margerida Lopez. These are some of the most hardworking principals and education thinkers I have ever known.

They boast track records of success in changing schools. These are among the finest South African educators when it comes to love for school and country. They are fiercely independent in their thinking and unsentimental in their ideas about the bottom line: the learning achievements of our children.

Mr President, I wait to hear from you.

The language of enthusiasm

Teachers need to buck up if our children are to prosper

13 October 2010

'Excuse me, colleagues, but did somebody die?' The bunch of teachers, sitting lazily on chairs around the barely furnished staff room looked decidedly morose, even depressed.

One was dozing off at this early hour of the day, just after 8 am. Another had her back half-turned to me – the motivational speaker brought in by the principal to 'say something encouraging to the staff'. A teacher in the corner held her head in her hands as if she had just witnessed a terrible tragedy from which she would never recover.

To make matters worse, this was the first day of the final term, the examinations term, we used to call it. This was also the first day of teaching after the long teachers' strike. One would have expected energy, enthusiasm, alertness, determination and a sense of panic as the examinations loomed. But I might as well have been in the Mangaung Cemetery in this sprawling township on the edges of the city of Bloemfontein.

I had just spoken to the 900 high school children outside in the already blazing heat of the early morning. We had whipped the young people into a frenzy of excitement for education and life. They responded with warmth and energy. These children came to school to learn, no doubt about it. In fact, this was one of the schools whose pupils stoned the Cosas marchers who tried to disrupt learning there; the poor disrupters were sent packing.

At this school, the children were dead serious about their futures. But there is a reason why the senior certificate pass rate at this school stands at about 40 per cent every year – the teachers.

I can hear the excuses, but here are the facts. No government on this continent spends more money on teacher development than South Africa. Almost the entire education budget goes to teacher salaries. Teachers enjoy job protection, regardless of the results of the children placed in their care – if all your learners fail, no need for concern, you cannot lose your job.

Back to the staff room. I try to motivate the teachers with a fascinating video clip in which a man responds to a dinner table question intended to embarrass him as a teacher among some rich professionals: 'Honestly, Dennis, what do you make?'

Dennis responds in anger: 'I make children spell correctly; I make them walk on air; I make parents see their children in ways they never did before; I make an underachiever reach the top of his class; you want to know what I make? I make a difference!'

Slowly the teachers rise from their state of near-slumber. Everybody is sitting up straight after five minutes. An 'amen' here and there. The message seems to be working.

I have absolutely no evidence for this claim, but I am prepared to bet that there is a relationship between a teacher's body language and the performance levels of her learners.

Children have a way of figuring out very quickly whether a teacher, or indeed any adult, is a fake. If your body language signals disinterest, tiredness or distress, they will know immediately that you care neither about your profession nor about your class of pupils.

I just hope no school pupil was watching the atrocious display of thuggish behaviour last week at the conference of one of our powerful teachers' unions.

Faced with the challenging remarks from a prominent politician that teachers strike and disrupt the poorest schools while their own offspring sit cotton-woolled in undisrupted former white schools, the unionists booed and prevented the man from speaking.

The truth hurts, for this is the ultimate act of selfishness: my children are okay, to hell with yours.

As we move towards the door of the staff room, I jump ahead of the teachers, demonstrating how one should enter your school and classroom every day.

Your body should signal intent, enthusiasm, interest in the subject and commitment to the learners. The spectacle would have been hilarious in any other context – the motivational speaker walking and leaping and praising kids, so to speak. As I looked behind me, a few other teachers came jumping as well.

In the new year, the University of the Free State is going to work with twenty schools, including this one, to ensure that the 900 children here and elsewhere are given a solid chance to make it in school and in life. We will do things differently from all other school interventions in South Africa.

Teachers and principals in every school will have an experienced mentor with a track record of success working alongside each of them. The first qualification of the mentor will be positive body language.

Something familiar in Flanders

SA doesn't have a monopoly on bridging great divides

29 September 2010

'We call them black schools,' says the chaperone taking me on a tour of schools and universities in Belgium. 'But we do not like this word "black".'

In one of the most tolerant countries in the world, I find two school systems.

One for recent, poor immigrants from Turkey, Albania, Romania, Poland, several North African states and even one or two children from South Africa. And another school system for well-off Belgian children – mainly from Flanders, the Flemish-speaking part of a rigidly divided country.

Here is the clearest example of how black has come to mean something other than skin colour. The poor European immigrant children are white and, if you insist, some a little brown, but certainly not black in the way we Africans think about it. Black, here and elsewhere, is a malaise, shorthand for trouble and those not fitting into the dominant cultures of the West, such as poor Muslim children from Turkey.

Belgium, like much of wealthy Europe, is struggling to cope with the influx (I use the word deliberately) of poor immigrants, which is growing at an alarming rate.

Every now and again there is a public crisis, such as the success at the polls of anti-immigrant right-wing movements, or the conflict over immigrant Muslim traditions, such as the wearing of the burqa in public, or the unhygienic settlements being established by gypsies crossing the borders. You can sense more serious trouble coming down the road as separate ethnic townships start to take root.

It took me at least a day before I realised where I was. 'This is the country that killed the hero of my angry youth,' I suddenly realised walking between government offices in Brussels. I raised the issue with my hosts.

'Well, he insulted our king,' said one on hearing the name Patrice Lumumba. Others saw this as the problem of a previous generation; the children are born free (sound familiar?) from responsibility for one of the worst models of colonialism in what the textbooks used to call the Belgian Congo. One foreign aid official was adamant: 'They had fifty years to get their act together and they messed it up' – meaning that the past is irrelevant, given such irresponsible behaviour on the part of the natives. Sound familiar?

'Go to the African museum (a place outside the capital city),' someone offered.

It is not an easy topic, and my emotional distress refuses to go away when I see a book of historical photographs showing Congolese appearing before colonial masters. Their hands have been chopped off (long before Sierra Leone's gangsters made this an art form), but their arms are tied needlessly in chains.

I want to know why Belgians are not as angry as South Africans. After all, here is a country where within minutes of meeting any Belgian they fly into an explanation of how the country is divided.

Flanders is the part that speaks Flemish, a language close to Dutch. Wallonia is the French-speaking part in the south. There is a small German-speaking part as well, but most talk only of the Flemish-French division. The more sophisticated among my informants insist this is a division in the mind only, and that there is only one Belgium.

It certainly feels as if their divisions are bloodless, and that there is constant compromise and accommodation – often achieved through financial concessions to the poorer French-speaking part – that keep the country together.

Bloodless, that is, until you meet the speaker of the Flemish parliament, an entertaining but pugnacious nationalist who volunteers over lunch that his wife recently climbed into a French-speaking citizen with her umbrella after the bloke insulted him.

According to newspapers in Flemish, the assailant took a swing at the speaker; according to newspapers in French, there was no such provocation. Still, their political fights are mainly harmless and the country will remain strongly united, even if the newspapers regularly headline a government about to collapse. Sound familiar?

'Every time there is talk of cession,' says my guide, 'Belgian flags go up around the country, especially in the capital.' I see the flag draped from some homes.

Then, a miracle. On the rough edges of the city there is a school filled with immigrants. The energetic principal has transformed it into a place of refuge marked by strong love for all the pupils and academic excellence. I watch the poor, black South African child joyfully darting with a ball among his peers on the handball court.

Back home, he would not stand a chance.

Walk on through the wind

Lessons for leadership

16 September 2010

Good morning, boys! What a privilege to be with you today. Since you find yourself at one of our best schools, you are all likely to be leaders in society.

You will have a great influence on many people. Some of you will create great companies, while others will teach generations of new citizens. Within this group there are future leaders who will become world-famous scholars, poets and engineers; there might be a Nobel Laureate in this group, or the person who will discover an Aids vaccine; and there may be among you those who will change whole countries. Since you are likely to be a leader, aided by what the school does, let me challenge you with three critical lessons that every successful leader must learn.

First, learn to cry.

In South Africa, we raise our boys to be aggressive. We take them through rugby drills and tell them to go to battle against the opposition. And so when a rugby player is confronted by a metro policeman, it is not enough to beat him, you must kill him; maybe the problem is that we call our sons Bees.

This is the original text of a less-structured speech delivered to the boys of St Stithians Boys' College in Randburg, Johannesburg, on Thursday, 9 September 2010.

We tell you, from a young age, not to cry. We mislead you by encouraging a 'stiff upper lip', something that belongs to another culture. This is wrong. Strong men cry; they share emotions.

Do not let anyone tell you that emotion is a woman's thing. I measure the strength of a boy by the extent to which he is connected to his inner self and not only to his base needs; by his consciousness of his brokenness, not only the faults of others; by his awareness that his strength lies in gentleness, not aggression.

Second, learn to love.

Look around you and you will see angry people everywhere. Men and women who hate. Many of us, black and white, speak only through our wounds. Past hurts imprison us, doing more harm to our own spirits and bodies than they do to the target of our hatreds. Strikers deliberately desert premature babies in paediatric emergency wards so that they die, in order to make a point about their salaries.

It is your generation that must take us beyond hate and indifference, to the love and embrace of others, especially of those whom we think are different from us.

Loving people who look like you is easy; expanding that embrace to those who appear different – the disabled, the foreign nationals from Africa, Muslims, black or white citizens – is the real measure of a man. In repairing what is wrong, we must reconcile what belongs together; do both at the same time.

Third, learn to stand alone.

South Africa consists of tribes. We do things in tribes; we hail the masses. What we feel, hear, fear or hope for is shaped by group thinking. David Harrison wrote a book called *White Tribe of Africa* to make this point. We often detest people who stand out.

Our culture reprimands children and adults alike who take a stand on principle. When you do this, you will lose some friends, but you will gain more respect. Peer pressure will try to force you to remain with the group; to side with the majority.

They might call you names, like 'racist' from one side, or *kafferboetie* from the other side. But when something is wrong, and when your conscience tells you there is a more noble way, take a stand and, if necessary, stand alone.

This is the story of Beyers Naudé who lost his pulpit, his people and his public life not too far from where your school is located.

On a dramatic Sunday he preached his last sermon, in which he said that the authority of God is higher than the authority of man. He told his wife: 'Whatever happens, we will be together.' He received a long banning order that restricted him to his home. He suffered death threats and was ostracised by his community.

But because he stood alone for what he believed was right, he helped bring us freedom, and now history and a whole nation judge him a hero.

This is how standing alone brings you back into community; maybe this is what the songwriters of the famous musical *Carousel* meant when they urged:

Walk on through the wind,
walk on through the rain,
though your dreams be
tossed and blown.
Walk on, walk on,
with hope in your heart
and you'll never walk alone;
you'll never walk alone.

May God bless you.

Those who can't, shouldn't teach

The effects of the teachers' strike on education

1 September 2010

The effects of the national strike on education are crystal clear. We know that more students will fail the senior certificate examination than would have been the case if the strike had been averted.

We know that when the Grade 12 results become known, poor black children will have suffered more than middle-class children in well-functioning schools with quality, dedicated teachers.

And we know that there will be knock-on effects for many students entering university in 2011, unprepared for higher learning.

From the perspective of a rural black child or an urban township schoolchild, the strike is an unmitigated disaster for a simple reason: it is in these poor and sometimes dysfunctional schools that instructional time matters much more towards the end of the school year as teachers play 'catch-up'.

In well-organised, well-off schools, alternative plans were made long before the strike took effect, and many teachers were already in revision mode as the terminal examinations approached.

That is what the public already knows. What really scares me about the strike are the invisible effects on teaching as a profession.

Thousands of children watch these strikes on television. They make little distinction between municipal workers overthrowing dirt bins, and teachers threatening and disrupting schools that put the learners first.

Many young people observing the mayhem would have harboured an interest in becoming teachers. What they see in the media will certainly turn the best among them away from teaching – what they see is not a profession, let alone a vocation. They witness anarchy, intimidation and disrespect.

No amount of bursary monies set aside especially for teachers, or appeals to their civic sense as young people, will draw thinking youth to a once-noble profession as its reputation lies shattered on the streets of South Africa.

It gets worse. The media reports with appreciation the fact that children are teaching children. The Department of Basic Education spends bags of money on adverts calling on the general public to assist in schools. There you have it: anyone can teach. What kind of nonsense is this? Small wonder no one takes the profession of teaching seriously.

Let me give an appropriate analogy. Let's assume all cardiac surgeons go on strike. They refuse to do heart surgery of any kind. A call goes out through the media for the public to come and help. Thousands of people send their curriculum vitae to the Department of Health, with school certificates and diplomas attached. Need I go any further?

Any sane person would find such calls for public assistance ridiculous. What makes you think anyone can step into a hospital theatre and perform heart surgery?

Anybody who has studied the science and art of teaching will tell you that the analogy is not as far-fetched as one might think. The complexity of the act of teaching, curriculum design, assessment measurement, classroom management or school leadership fills the pages of scholarly books around the world.

But as so many of us confuse teaching with simply uttering words in front of a classroom of learners – what the heck, any idiot can do it. And since the bloody damage of a heart operation gone wrong is obviously more visible, who cares about the invisible damage done to young minds when just anyone shows up to teach?

It is, therefore, not only the destructive behaviour of some of the striking teachers that turns off otherwise idealistic youth from becoming teachers; it is also the messages we send in how the strike is managed, especially when we applaud children teaching children and motor mechanics and chartered accountants showing up at the classroom door.

I am certainly not suggesting that qualified professionals in other fields cannot be taught to become teachers. In fact, this is highly desirable in fields such as engineering or economics. But, as any student who has sat through university classes will attest to, just because the professor is a good scientist in the laboratory does not mean he or she can teach.

Most of our teachers are not like the marauding hooligans going from school to school to make sure all children suffer. Many of our teachers are decent, hard-working professionals. There are many such teachers in the poorest schools of the country, who desperately try to uphold the standards of the profession.

A principal wrote to me this past week. She is black, poorly paid and heads a school under very challenging conditions. She has been threatened and abused for not participating in the strike. But she stands strong: 'The children come first.'

The kids are going to be okay

Inspiration from South African schoolchildren

4 August 2010

If you have ever harboured any doubts about South Africa having a bright and prosperous future, this past week would have blown you away.

After speaking to young South Africans in high schools from Potchefstroom and Klerksdorp in the dry north-western regions of the country, to the idyllic town of Paarl in the Boland and Rondebosch in suburban Cape Town, I can assure you that you can relax. It will go well with us.

Geesie Theron is much smaller and leaner than her twin sister at DF Malan High School. You quickly forget the troubled name of the school when you meet this amazing young South African. I stretch out my hand to greet the small teenager, but there is no response.

The young woman is blind, a condition brought on by an inoperable tumour on her brain. It would be a mistake to feel sorry for Geesie, or to rush to embrace her – I made both.

Within seconds, Geesie took over the conversation and with an unbelievable optimism and zest for life told me about hope, determination and the learning that comes through suffering. I could literally feel the goose bumps rise on my brown skin.

The night before I had addressed the Paarl Youth Initiative, a project by farmers in the Boland to invest heavily in extracurricular learning opportunities, mainly for the children of farm labourers.

From Grade 8, farm children are exposed to writing, museums, life skills, career preparation, public speaking and other kinds of confidence-building activities. And it shows. The first Grade 12 group to come through this programme received me, and introduced me to the community packed into a hall on the lower end of the Paarl Main Road, long after one has passed the fancy rich schools.

All those images of farmers who abuse their labourers – that singularly misleading narrative of white-black relationships on farms – exploded into mythology as I watched these proud, confident and highly articulate black teenagers present themselves on the platform.

Rarely had I ever seen such youthful promise and potential anywhere in the world. For a few moments, while standing before the audience, I could not speak. I sipped some water to conceal the lump-in-the-throat feeling.

Onto one of South Africa's most distinguished public high schools. I was awaiting my time to speak, when a young man with one hand in his pocket strolled over to me completely oblivious – unlike most teenagers – of his peer group watching.

'Are you Professor Jansen?' he asked with an easy confidence one would seldom find among Grade 10 children, even here at Westerford High School.

'Yes, I am,' I said chirpily, with what he must have read as a bemused smile. But the real shock came with his next words. Leaning back slightly, he took his time to say this: 'I would like to thank you for defusing that racial situation there at the University of the Free State!'

He did not grovel and he was not intimidated. Nor did he cross the thin line between confidence and arrogance, like so many self-assured kids whose parents have too much money.

Too often the media narrows our focus on political youth – those angry, bitter and unreflective young men who dominate the public discourse in South Africa. They are a minority whose passions are fuelled by adults in major political parties; they have no ambitions for education (let alone service), but place their only hope of income on political positions and the scavenger opportunities that come with such elevation. That is why their meetings are so violent, their language so spiteful and their contests so intense. It's not simply about positions; it's about *pap*.

Look beyond this motley crew.

There are millions of young people in our school systems who are decent, respectful and idealistic about their country and its future.

They behave like the teenagers described in the stories above. They want something to look forward to but, more importantly, they want to be the difference that they seek in their land.

The last word goes to Zama, a beautiful and composed young woman who was adopted into a large, loving family.

I saw her years ago, at the end of a long nightmare of neglect and abuse. But she had worked her way through school into university, studying biological sciences.

Tears streamed down her face when she heard that she would now be able to study medicine at a leading university in the middle of the country.

Practice makes perfect pupils

Education doesn't need a quick fix, it needs dedication

28 July 2010

Y ou do not want to find yourself in Springfontein in winter. I suspect the founders of this rural town in the southern Free State called the place by this name because one literally has to *spring* (jump) around simply to keep warm.

Nor do you want to find yourself in a Springfontein primary school where, to my shock, I find small children inside thin-walled prefab buildings with asbestos roofs to kill you. Shivering, I slip into one of the classrooms. The children are all thin as sticks, a sure sign of the abject poverty of the area.

One adult after another whispers the words 'fetal alcohol syndrome', in reference to a malady that apparently afflicts many of these precious souls. In all my years of visiting schools in southern Africa, this is the worst I have ever seen.

Worst, that is, until you enter the classroom of Mrs Le Roux. The teacher is not there, and so I am puzzled by the fact that every child among the thirty or so pupils is frantically busy writing. This is rare in most schools – an absent teacher is an invitation to party, but not here in Springfontein. There is nothing much in this classroom, except for some bright posters on the walls. But every desk has a small pot filled with sharpened pencils, and writing books that are clearly overused by South African standards.

I am intrigued by the bulging writing books, all neatly covered. And then the next shock. As I page through a sample of the books I notice that they are filled with neat children's handwriting on every page. Even more surprising is the fact that every writing page has been marked by the teacher and, after five or so pages, there appears an assessment score (8 out of 10, for example) with a bright, smiling face and a personal word of encouragement in the teacher's pen.

'This teacher does not sleep,' I said to myself. It was hardly the middle of the school year and each writing book was almost full already.

Then the teacher burst into the room. Her face lit up as she recognised her visitors and she apologised for being out of class for a few minutes. I asked her how she managed to get children to do so much writing so early in the year. 'Oh,' she said, 'that is their third writing book for the term.'

No need to worry in this classroom about the damage wrought by outcomes-based education. This teacher has practised the foundation skills of writing every day to a point that the children so obviously enjoyed putting pen to paper to write, compose, imagine and communicate.

The cold, hunger and asbestos notwithstanding, these children have a huge advantage over most South African youth. As someone who has taught in at least three South African universities, I can honestly say that I saw much more thoughtful and language-correct writing in this primary school than among many undergraduate students. It is called 'practise, practise, practise'. The lack of writing practice lies behind much of the rot in our education system.

Young children and older students struggle with communication and imagination, because the practice of writing is not firmly established in primary schools through to universities.

Students no longer write long and challenging essays; rather, we give them multiple-choice questionnaires to assess their knowledge in a particular field. I understand that such papers are more efficient when teaching and managing large classes, but they come at a huge cost when overused at the expense of writing practice. They are also a nice cop-out for the lazy teacher who would rather not mark long essays.

I am thinking of proposing to my university senate that our admissions processes include the requirement that prospective students write a ten-page essay on an assigned topic so that we can obtain a more complete picture of their ability to succeed in a tough academic environment. A student's writing tells you about his or her organisational abilities, emotional capacity, literary insight, persuasive powers and, of course, communication skills. Writing reveals more than language competence.

Mrs Le Roux will not be joining the possible strike by thousands of teachers if their union does not get their way with demanding more money. She recognises that keeping these desperately poor, thin and vulnerable children writing is the one shot they have to get out of their miserable circumstances.

Oh, by the way, the teacher is white and Afrikaans-speaking. The children are all black.

The enduring legacy of OBE

The hidden damage to our education system

21 July 2010

One dark winter's night in late 1998 a group of political heavyweights came to my office in Durban with the simple agenda of threatening me. I had just published an essay titled, 'Ten reasons why OBE will fail'.

A national conference was organised shortly afterwards with the agenda of taking apart the critic rather than his argument, through a scathing presentation by an academic comrade, now deceased.

If the disastrous consequences of outcomes-based education had been visible on television in the form of millions of sick and dying children, we would be horrified by the effects of this experiment of our first democratic government. But since wounds in education are not as visible as those in a health crisis, we cannot immediately see the damage wrought.

The sheer dishonesty among politicians and unionists after Minister of Basic Education, Angie Motshekga, announced the obvious – that OBE was dead – was on the one hand, amusing and, on the other hand, disturbing. A former Minister of Education told a newspaper that the current Minister of Education was to blame; the latter claimed that he was not the one with the power to decide on OBE. A prominent education personality denied that he was the father of OBE. A union official joined the fray and said his organisation had always been opposed to OBE.

The rampant denialism reminded me of National Party politicians in the mid-1990s; none of them had ever supported apartheid ...

But what are the not-so-obvious damages of OBE? I can think of six.

First, there are the costs to the country in financial terms. Hundreds of millions of rand were spent on training teachers, developing materials, preparing curriculum facilitators, hiring international experts, commissioning expensive reviews and evaluations, writing and rewriting learning guides, arranging conferences, and on and on.

Second, there are opportunity costs; that is, the things we could have done in the past twelve years to build a new school system founded on a strong curriculum that established the foundations of reading, writing and thinking in the early years. That 'window of opportunity' is forever lost as we now try to undo the intertwined damage of apartheid and OBE.

Third, there are motivational costs to be reckoned. The early years of democracy were a time of excitement and expectation; the system was ready for, and open to, change. Teachers understood that the apartheid curriculum had to go; they geared themselves for change. Many embraced OBE, often clumsily so, as the remedy to apartheid knowledge. Now they will not believe us as easily again. There is exhaustion among professional teachers, many of whom feel they have been duped.

Fourth, there are legacy costs. One myth about dramatic curriculum changes is that a senior official, like a Minister, can make an announcement and an unwanted curriculum simply disappears. The problem is that OBE is settled in the consciousness of most of our teachers; it will continue to reflect in their patterns of teaching and assessing; it remains in the organisation of classrooms. Just like apartheid knowledge lingers in the teaching practices of many schools, so OBE will continue to influence negatively what teachers and learners actually do in their classrooms for a long time to come.

Fifth, there have been, and will be, economic costs. Fewer and fewer students, with or without post-school training, have been capable of being absorbed into the marketplace. It would be interesting to ask an education economist to calculate the costs to the economy of OBE in terms of the trained labour we did not produce.

Sixth, and most importantly, there are serious human costs. Children already disadvantaged were exposed to a curriculum that made a fragile learning environment worse. Instead of learning those vital competencies of reading, writing and calculating, they were exposed to high-brow constructivist theories that kept many of them illiterate. Those effects not only forced many to leave the school system; they also pushed weaker and weaker students into universities where they again struggled to succeed.

There should, of course, be political costs. Heads should roll. The architects of OBE are very much among us today – some have left the Department of Education for

the private sector; others run universities; a few have retired; and many simply shifted from one government department to the next. Here's the sad news: the arrogance in
our political system means that none of these people will
be held accountable.

Matric exam failing the test

Stress and uncertainty for Mpumalanga matrics

6 January 2010

Put yourself in the shoes of a 2009 matriculant from Mpumalanga.

You had to wait longer than ever before for your matric results to be released. You suffered through Christmas worrying: 'Did I pass; did I pass well enough; will I pass the mathematics paper which everybody agrees was too difficult?' And much of your holiday was spent with nagging doubts about your results.

Eventually, 7 January 2010 arrives and then you hear on television that the results for your province will be delayed by yet another period because of doubts about the credibility of the examination marks in your region.

Your further problem is that on 8 January, the day following the release of the results, the new first-year class will be officially welcomed by the rector and staff of the University of the Free State. Do you attend, in the hope that you will eventually pass and meet the criteria for acceptance into medical school? Or will you be wasting your time and money travelling all that way, only to find out some time later that you did not pass well enough after all? Your nerves are wracked, your parents are in a panic, and your friends from other provinces call you ecstatically to share their results.

I wonder whether examination administrators and education department officials really think about the impact such delays in the release of results have on young people. I wonder if anyone has calculated the costs of these delays on the university application and entry decisions that young people and their families have to make.

It is now clear that Mpumalanga province has neither the managerial capacity nor the ethical backbone to run a competent and clean matriculation examination. Not one, but five papers were leaked; not only in 2009, but in previous years as well. There is only one solution in the short term. The national Department of Education should run the examinations in Mpumalanga, or hand over this function to a competent and established private provider such as the Independent Examinations Board.

I know, handing over this responsibility to an independent and private provider will raise the ideological hackles of some, but we need to be pragmatic here: 60 000 matriculants now live in uncertainty and stress because of repeated failures to manage a high-stakes examination in this province.

The administrative and financial consequences of such a delay are already enormous. But, most of all, citizen confidence in a state-sponsored examination remains low and this is not good for the government or for public schools. Drastic and immediate action is needed.

The national government clearly needs to retain the oversight function for examinations, but the administration of the matric examination has to shift to a competent authority. One province cannot be allowed to cast doubt on the credibility of a national examination system. Such decisive action on the part of the Minister of Basic Education will be an indication of firm leadership in a crisis, and would augur well for building public confidence in the department.

In the meantime, we need to reopen a national discussion on whether the senior certificate examination is still the best way to decide on university entrance. Universities already have their own complex of entrance tests and decisions that weigh them down. One reason for this is the lack of confidence in the school examinations alone as a predictor of success at university.

It is time to end this complex and burdensome testing system. School-leaving examinations should end with a school-leaving certificate and a school-based examination. Then there should be a single university-entrance examination for those who wish to apply to university, and a similar entrance test for colleges. These examinations for university entrance could be held in June of the year preceding first-year studies. Instantly, the corruption and incompetence will fall away, and the stress and uncertainty end for all students, especially those in Mpumalanga.

Happy schools aren't a myth

Boshoff High School sets a shining example

21 April 2010

To get to Boshoff High School you have to slow down as you enter the little town by the same name, and navigate unpredictable twists and turns to avoid the gaping potholes that mark all the rural roads in the Free State.

The town itself is dead; there is little evidence of human life in the late morning, except for two or three men huddled together here or there, with no particular need to be anywhere soon.

From the point where you enter the town, you can see the point ahead of you where you exit the town after a slight rise in the road. It is as if a volcanic eruption recently happened nearby and cleared out this little town in the middle of nowhere. Suddenly, a bright board jumps out at you while you narrowly avoid another pothole.

It says 'Boshoff High School', and whatever idea you had of the town is about to be exploded.

We enter through the narrow gate and what strikes us are the scores of neatly dressed students spread across the school grounds and behind them, unmistakably, the school principal. He waves us in; we're about to have the ride of our lives.

My senses tell me there is something unusual about this school. This is the first time in my life, after having visited thousands of schools across the length and breadth of this beautiful country, that I have witnessed such a happy school. Every single child wears a bright, smiling face.

In high schools, this is rare. Children look depressed. Teachers look worn out; boys and girls look tired all the time. And to demonstrate signs of life as a teenager is to be decidedly uncool. But in these hallways and in the school hall, outside on the school grounds and inside the principal's office, everybody exudes happiness.

The last time I saw such unprovoked happiness was in a psychiatric ward. I become suspicious ...

The hall is packed with senior students, all smiling broadly – and I haven't even spoken yet. I discard my jacket, don the University of the Free State marketing hat, and let rip with familiar themes of hard work, persistence and the importance of going to university. There was, of course, only one university worth considering, as I rattled off the list of innovations about to make a good university great. Smiles throughout.

The mandatory jokes at the beginning of the speech have some of the boys scaling the walls in laughter and girls falling from their chairs in delight.

The expression 'happy school' is an example I regularly use to explain the word 'oxymoron'. Not here at Boshoff High.

The research literature speaks about school climate. It refers to the atmosphere in a school; the way children and teachers feel about the school; the way the school is organised to promote a positive learning and living environment. A positive school climate is about a joyful place where people simply want to be.

Boshoff High School is a poor, former white school where most of the students are black. The principal, the leader of this joyful school, is remarkable. Not a single complaint. He sees his duty as being the leader of positive thinking in the school. Problems are challenges, not liabilities. And it shows in the attitudes of his learners.

Children come from every one of the nine provinces to be at Boshoff. They cannot remember when last a child failed matric in this school where most of the learners are, of necessity, boarders on the property.

This is the first school in which I could not find a piece of paper lying around. The hallways are perfectly polished. Bright signs meet you as you enter the hallways – the signs are uplifting, encouraging and speak of elevated goals for learning and for life.

Why, oh why, do our school principals and teachers in the rest of the country believe that the only way to achieve success is to make schooling miserable?

Why are we surprised that pupils are dull and depressed when schools are run by quasi-prison warders whose most common expressions are: 'Don't', or 'you will be in trouble if' or 'I am warning you that ...'?

Go to a school assembly and listen carefully to the number of times principals and teachers threaten children. It will scare you.

At Boshoff High you discover that you can have school discipline and academic success at the same time, and have a whole lot of fun getting there.

The Lord of the Flies' legions

An angry youth protest, a warning for the future?

24 March 2010

Thousands of children stream out of Soweto schools onto the streets in protests. Police confront them with rubber bullets and a water cannon.

The swelling numbers of students leave the classrooms to demand justice. They are met with the full force of mounted police and armed vehicles. Soweto 1976?

No, Soweto 2010. The fight against apartheid education? No, no, no – the students are surrounding the police cells and magistrate's court where another young man and his fellow drag-racing driver are being held in a police station for allegedly mowing down six school pupils, killing four and maiming two.

Did the students leave school to mourn the loss of their friends and to see justice take its course in the courts of a democratic South Africa?

No, their posters make it clear that they came to kill the man with the curious name of Jub Jub.

It is impossible to measure the depth of despair and desperation and the loss of the families of those killed in this senseless act of murder (as the charge sheet alleges) by two drag-racing drivers who, it is also alleged, were high on illegal substances.

One can only imagine the pain of losing fellow matriculants, sitting at their desks next to you in school one day and only a few days later being lowered into dusty graves, never to be seen again.

The anger of families, school mates and the community is understandable.

That said, take another look at the series of photographs and video-streams of our young people in Soweto. For, if you look carefully, you will see your future and the future of your country. And when you do that, be afraid – be very afraid.

These are not 'learners', as official policy documents of the government's education departments have so euphemistically called post-apartheid youth. These are potential killers. Their logic is simple: you kill our friends; we kill you.

I have absolutely no doubt that if that crowd of young people were to lay hands on Jub Jub and his fellow accused, they would be physically torn apart by the rage of these vengeful teenagers.

It is not only what happened in Soweto that should concern us. In the growing number of service delivery protests the youthfulness of the protestors should scare us.

They are not at school; they are manning the barricades. They dodge bullets and the police. Some of them are armed with rocks and more deadly projectiles. This is not about the legitimacy of the protests; that is another debate.

What concerns me as a teacher and a citizen is something much more serious, namely that we are breeding a new generation of youthful South Africans who are learning early to be angry, deadly angry, without adult intervention and without political or pedagogical correction.

Take another look, South Africa. This is your future. Yes, these young people are 'learning' – but not the rhythms of aerobic respiration or the construction of line graphs. They are learning to kill on instinct. They are learning to bypass judicial processes, and to demand instant justice.

They might have a reason, of course, to distrust the law – after all, you can kill and maim and still, as in this case, be released on bail of a mere R10 000. But that, too, is another debate, for on the streets of South Africa something horrible is happening, something much more devastating than any teacher in a disciplined school could ever produce.

We are producing and reproducing (yes, that's the word) a new generation of cold, callous, clinically dangerous youths who will not be in training or employment. They may slay a family for a television set, or shoot a pedestrian for a cellphone. They may rape and walk, not run, away.

Our finest historians will tell you dangerous behaviour does not just happen. Communities do not simply snap and start wiping out foreigners. This deadly behaviour comes from deep within our history and (here's the bad news) it is carried intergenerationally unless there is drastic intervention that breaks or interrupts the rhythms of destructive actions.

There are role models for angry, bitter and vengeful youth. Student organisations that once bore proud anti-apartheid credentials have morphed into something sinister and pernicious while unfairly drawing on (and sullying) the reputations of earlier movements of the same name.

It is no longer enough to keep young people in school for, as in the case of these Soweto youths, it is in school that they learn to be bitter and organise to be vengeful.

Take another look at our young people. You have been warned.

New school of thinking needed

Our government can't change our schools

10 March 2010

It is time to concede an unpleasant fact: our government does not have the capacity or the courage to change our schools in vast parts of this country.

Tens of thousands of students exit the school system between Grades 1 and 12. Half or more fall at the final hurdle, the matriculation examinations. Thousands pass matric poorly and end up without a job, outside of training and with no prospects of changing their situation. This much we know.

The problem is that the crisis is deepening.

One does not have to be a prophet to see the social upheaval and community disintegration that lie ahead as these angry, alienated youngsters begin to turn on each other and on ordinary citizens, in even more alarming numbers and with greater viciousness than we are witnessing at the moment.

Across the world, governments are responsible for schools. I like that. The term 'public schools' has deep meaning for me, for it suggests a broader ownership of schools that lies beyond the rather more restricting words, 'government schools'.

Public schools point to public values to be carried through these vital institutions called schools. Both my children went to public schools as a matter of principle; this is something we as parents are very proud of.

But what happens when those charged with funding, developing and supporting public schools on the part of the community – the government – fail to deliver? What if the schools under the control of the government fail the poorest of the poor?

What if one state examination after another simply reinforces the fact that there is no change in the performance of young people, whether in the foundational grades of primary school or in the terminal grades of high school?

What if there is no end in sight to the misery of public schooling? Then it is time to consider the possibility that these schools should be taken over by outside agencies.

South Africa would not be the first country in which corporations take over schools. They bring a different culture. They apply the logic of the bottom line, which in this case would include student achievement.

Corporations have a handle on strong managerial processes that, in their context, move efficiently from conceptualisation to execution to results.

True, this would not be an ideal cultural fit for schools that have more collegiate, educational cultures. But if they produce the results, let leading businesspersons or groups take over a hundred of the most dysfunctional schools in, say, the Eastern Cape, and we'll see whether we get better results.

Some teachers and principals will not like this, because it unsettles the inertia or steady state of institutions that have long lost their energy and vitality. But I am convinced parents would love it and, even more importantly, students will be attracted towards business-operated schools because their chances in life will improve dramatically for the first time.

What about some universities taking over fifty of the worst-performing schools in their province? Let them take the responsibility for on-site teacher training; for direct career counselling and subject choices in Grade 10 and upwards; for co-mobilising resource support for the schools; for leadership direction and giving support to the principal.

Once again, such a move is not unprecedented in other parts of the world where strong university-school partnerships exist.

Go further and have some of the larger churches take over schools.

After all, before that pernicious decision of the new apartheid state to strangle ecclesiastical schools in the 1950s, it was Catholic and Anglican schools, among others, that produced the black elite who became the learning citizens of South Africa and its neighbours.

The government, predictably, will be incensed by such a proposal. It suggests a bail-out, an acknowledgment of defeat, a lack of trust in the ability of the state to deliver on election promises.

But the government will always have schools to run. How about sharing that responsibility and taking the credit for success?

After all, when tens of thousands of students in well-resourced private schools do well, this is good for the country, the economy and democracy.

Star awards: The rebel alliance

Challenging convention is essential for success

24 February 2010

Being a veteran of high school awards evenings, this was the one award that blew me away. This Randburg school had a preschool attached to a primary school that fed into a high school – all on the same expansive property.

Before it was my turn to speak, the awards were distributed with the usual spread, from best sportsman to best academic student.

Then came the shock: an award was given to a student for not having missed a single day in school from his first day in pre-school to his last day in matric.

When my turn came to speak, I called the scrawny young man forward and asked him to return the award.

'I have two questions for you,' I told the slightly amused young fellow. 'I have a question about your immune system, and I have a question about your sanity.' How on earth does a child not miss a day out of fourteen years of schooling?

I firmly believe that for children to become successful adults in a demanding world, they have to learn how to break some rules. Challenging convention is fundamental to success in competitive economies.

I have been fortunate to meet several Nobel Laureates in my lifetime, and the one thing I know for certain is that they do not follow an established algorithm.

They learn the rules, and then they break them. This is the key to creativity and innovation. It is the story of Bill Gates and Richard Branson, as it is the story of Desmond Tutu and Mamphela Ramphele.

Imagine how boring flying would be were it not for the irreverence of Mr Branson and his Virgin Atlantic Airlines. Imagine what kind of country we might have had were it not for Desmond Tutu defying apartheid's labyrinth of rules and regulations in favour of a higher set of values.

Imagine what kind of transition we might have had if Nelson Mandela came out of prison on the terms of P.W. Botha – to first renounce violence.

The reason I once attacked the wearing of school uniforms had nothing to do with the uniform as an item of clothing; it had everything to do with the uniform thinking that schools impose on children. The kind of thinking that keeps a boy glued to his desk for fourteen years.

Now I go around the country and tell children in well-ordered public schools to break the rules. I tell them to break through the fence at least once in their school career and run away for a day.

See what happens when you overheat a test tube. Come to school with your underpants on the outside (after all, who said it should be on the inside?)

Stand on your head in the history classroom at the very moment the teacher launches into the origins of the Great Trek.

Solve a mathematics problem on the board by starting with the solution and working backwards; that is, in defiance of the conventional logic of problem solving.

In other words, land in trouble at least once. You will never understand how a system functions (including a school system) unless you throw a spanner in the works, someone once said.

This is why, as a university teacher, I cannot trust matric results. It tells me about students who follow convention, who can stay up all night and memorise the facts, who can do exactly what the teacher tells them and pass the examinations.

I know from experience that the students who do well at university have a C-average. They never win those mindless school awards because they think for themselves. They take more time in their studies because they weigh alternatives.

The modern workplace does not do well with automatons.

Employers tell us time after time that they are on the lookout for original thinkers; for young people who respond well to unexpected situations, who can solve original problems in the workplace, who think for themselves.

I therefore do not ask young people to rebel just for the heck of it; I am asking them to change their pattern of thinking, and to alter their disposition towards rules and authority.

I am very grateful to a Pretoria high school for agreeing to give an award that I had proposed. This award now features regularly on award night. It is for the student who respects people, but who breaks the rules carefully. The citation reads: 'One for whom convention is a burden.'

The parlous state of our nation

Empty promises for education

17 February 2010

Strange how the values your parents taught you come back to memory in a crisis. So as I thought of President Zuma's travails, the words of my late father kept running through my head: 'Don't kick a man when he's down.'

With this in mind, I took some time to decide whether or not I would critically take on the education proposals in the recent state-of-the-nation address.

Then I realised that these were not President Zuma's personal views; the speech is the collective statement of hordes of bureaucrats and politicians, of political advisers and interest groups – the government. In other words, it's not simply about the president.

So here goes: There was nothing in the education promises in the state-of-the-nation address that remotely began to deal with the critical factors that are keeping the school system in permanent crisis. Let's take the promises one by one:

- 'We will improve the ability of our children to read, write and count in the foundation years.'

    Exactly how will this happen? We have had all kinds of government and NGO initiatives since the early 1990s to do exactly this, and there is every indication from existing tests that things have grown worse, let alone stayed the same. This was a policy aim of previous Ministers; the brutal fact is that nothing has worked to shift the system towards improved performance in the foundation years.

And when you can count on one hand the number of African students in foundation programmes in teacher education at our universities, there is nothing to suggest that improved mother-tongue instruction is possible.

- 'We want pupils and teachers in class, on time, learning and teaching for seven hours a day.'

We all want this. In fact, this is what teachers and principals get paid to do. But simply expressing such a desire will not change anything.

The forces (including powerful teachers' unions) that keep students and teachers out of school are far more powerful than any instruments (legal or political) that the government has in its arsenal to reverse a situation in which most of our children receive less than 50 per cent of the instructional time listed on the timetable.

- 'We will assist teachers by producing detailed lesson plans.'

Wait a minute. Is this not what teachers were trained to do on day one of their four-year teacher training programmes? What kind of teacher cannot develop a lesson plan? How can a detailed lesson plan in one school simply apply across the cultural, resource and linguistic contexts of another school? What does this do to teacher autonomy and professionalism when the state develops your lesson plans in detail?

This is extremely dangerous.

- 'All Grade 3, 6 and 9 students will write independently moderated literacy and numeracy tests.'

    Somebody should have told the president this has been happening for years in provinces like the Western Cape. They should also have told the president that despite years of such testing, the results look worse.

    What one does with the test results can make a difference, but there is every indication that, at provincial and national level, there is no planning and operational capacity or insight to do so.

- 'Pass rates in literacy and numeracy will increase from the current range of 25–40 per cent to 60 per cent.'

    The problem with 2014 is that there will be a new government and nobody to hold this government accountable for the results not being achieved. How can this dramatic increase in literacy and numeracy be achieved on a system-wide basis? Why has this scale of improvement in test results not happened in a province with the most favourable resource profile, namely the Western Cape?

- 'A total of 27 000 schools will be assessed by officials from the Department of Education.'

    Please. Even if there existed the political will to do this over the heads of the teachers' unions, where will the human resources and financial capacity to achieve this come from? Even with the best plans of a programme called Whole School Evaluation, only a fraction of the schools in a province could be accessed.

- '175 000 students will gain university admission passes by 2014.'

  I have no idea where this number came from, but this means another 65 000 Grade 12 students qualifying for university. See all of the reasons above why this is another impossible goal for a school system that's on its knees.

Ethembeni breaks the mould

A simple recipe for school success

10 February 2010

I simply did not believe the principal when she made the announcement: 'For the past twelve years, no child in this school has failed matric.'

I would not readily believe that kind of claim from any top-notch school in the country; I certainly found it difficult to believe at the Ethembeni Enrichment Centre, situated in a rundown area of Port Elizabeth.

Nothing in the school suggested that the children had a fair chance. The school building was dilapidated and the classrooms were barely furnished. The driveway to the school was a rocky, narrow passage that one could exit only by reversing.

The school hall was packed with a few hundred eager faces, the children virtually sitting on top of one other on the floor.

As I studied each face from the makeshift platform that accommodated some of the teachers and my recruiting team from the university, I saw struggle, hunger and poverty etched into each child's countenance. No, for any child to pass under these difficult circumstances would take a miracle.

But a miracle is what we got.

Suddenly, in this drab building packed with human bodies, the children started to sing. They came alive with joy, dancing and laughter as one of the senior girls led the singing. The moving rendition of *The Lord's Prayer* in isiXhosa brought tears to the eyes of my colleagues. This was goose-bump stuff.

As visitors, we were all moved by the spirit of the school as teachers praised pupils and as pupils welcomed the visitors. We joined in the uplifting songs and danced with the children. Something was going on here that I did not see in some of the plush schools of the Eastern Cape.

How did the teachers and the principal create this high-spirited learning environment? The answer was, as usual, disarmingly simple, and was reflected in what the school calls 'non-negotiables', the specifics of which were pasted onto the walls:

- Class attendance is compulsory.
- Students must be punctual.
- Students must complete all given homework.
- Students must keep the school grounds neat and tidy.
- Parental involvement is essential.

There you are; nothing complex. Nothing requiring millions of rands and nothing requiring years of research. And no handwringing nonsense about if children were taught in their indigenous tongue, academic results would improve.

'Our medium of instruction is English,' says the school brochure, pure and simple.

A simple set of commitments is all one needs to change a school. Here there is no need to instruct teachers on what to do; the rules are about the responsibility of parents and students.

What really fascinated me was the motto of the school: 'Avoid the soft option.'

The message was clear that Ethembeni was not going to pander to the new ideology of schooling in South Africa, namely to lower expectations so that students can pass with less than 50 per cent in some subjects and score ridiculously high marks in that meaningless subject, life orientation.

This school worked with the fundamental principle of good education: when you demand high standards of children, they rise to meet those standards, irrespective of their socio-economic circumstances. Expect little from pupils and they will perform accordingly.

Once a finishing school for second-chance pupils, Ethembeni is now one of the top three of more than seventy schools in the Port Elizabeth district, ranking alongside very expensive schools in the area. One student obtained 100 per cent in Grade 12 mathematics.

One external expert noted: 'Ethembeni has broken the mould of failure, disillusionment, apathy and (sometimes) anarchy' of many township schools.

Yes, of course, the school still needs curtains, paint, laboratories, sanding and varnishing of floors, and decent ablution blocks. It needs teaching materials.

But what it already has is priceless: dedicated teachers, spirited pupils, involved parents – and a determination to succeed.

'Ethembeni' means 'place of hope'.

Learn us how to talk proper

Poor language communication can damage life chances

3 February 2010

Spend some time at a good school and, sooner or later, you will hear a senior teacher say something like: 'Every teacher is a language teacher.'

What this means is that not only the English or Afrikaans or Zulu language teachers influence the language competencies of students, all teachers do.

The language usage of a science or history teacher matters as much as that of the English teacher teaching the rules of grammar and composition.

This is a crucial point in a country in which schoolchildren, young and old, fare poorly in literacy and communication. It is a disadvantage that shows up in alarming ways in their undergraduate years at university. The truth is that, of the nine or ten periods in a school day, most of the time is taken up by non-language specialists.

Most of our high school pupils learn about momentum in science, and about the Holocaust in history, through the medium of English. The teacher's language usage impresses on the child right and wrong ways of using language and, over a period of twelve years, the cumulative effects of poor language communication can do huge damage to the life chances of the school leaver.

Language learning, of course, happens much earlier. Listen to a child of four or five whose use of language is ordered and precise, and you will find a parent whose use of language is ordered and precise.

Conversely, listen to parents who punctuate their sentences with swearwords and the careless use of language – the child will speak the same way. Correct language usage is not only the school's problem; it is also a responsibility of parents.

And nothing irritates me more than listening to TV newsreaders. Some event is quickly announced and then you hear the following irritating expression: 'This, as the African Union decried the horrors of Haiti.'

Excuse me: 'This, as ...'? What kind of idiotic contortion of language is that? There are millions of viewers watching the news, including children. You can bet many of them will write school essays starting with this clumsy construction: 'This, as ...'

Listen carefully to politicians speaking. Listen to prominent businesspeople communicating. Listen to – these are my favourites – sports personalities.

Can you hear Ali or Jeremy talking about 'clicket'? Listen to rugby coaches (you know who I mean) and commentators speaking, and you will find a disastrous English lesson for every young person watching.

No wonder I found it difficult at the three South African universities at which I taught to identify a youngster who could write a paragraph containing fewer than five or six grammatical errors.

Small wonder our young people cannot speak correctly and with confidence in a public conversation or debate. Speaking badly in English is contagious. In fact, I sometimes find myself slipping into the language use of my students, who regularly say things like: 'I am having a problem'. Indeed, you have a serious one, my friend.

Do not misconstrue what I am arguing for here. I am strongly opposed to any notion of a 'Queen's English' or some transported, fake-accented English that pretends to be what and where it is not.

But there is correct English, and there is wrong English. 'I am having a problem' is wrong and 'I have a problem' is right. 'This, as ...' should condemn the speaker to be kept after school to learn to speak and write properly, lest he become a mindless TV newsreader.

The way one uses language as a graduate makes a big difference in the job marketplace. We all know that a prospective employee, fresh out of high school or university, is not selected because of his or her knowledge of the life cycle of the fern or the reproductive habits of the garden snail. Nine times out of ten, candidates are chosen for their ability to communicate well in a major language.

There, I've got it off my chest; I've wanted to complain about our language use for some time now. This, as I prepare to go to bed.

From gangland to campus

Ordinary people changing lives

4 November 2009

The fifty-nine Grade 7 pupils about to board the bus were tired. They had just had an exhausting educational tour through Bloemfontein, Pretoria and Johannesburg, and were on their way back to the Cape Flats past the Big Hole in Kimberley.

I wondered in amazement at how my friends and colleagues had volunteered their time and energy to make this remarkable event possible.

Some gave of their money, others gave of their talent; all of them gave support. As the bus revved up to leave, one boy turned back and came towards me. With gold chains around his neck, his slinking style reminded me of my days on the Flats: you walk as if there is something wrong with your vertebral column, with your shoulders falling ahead of you in alternate waves.

My mind raced back to the Flats, where I grew up. These were the type of fellows your mother warned you about with the certainty of parents who could tell who the good kids were and whom to avoid.

As I sized the young man up I saw something in his face that spelt hardship, and I was curious about why he would risk being 'uncool', coming to talk to me as fifty-eight pairs of eyes stared out of the bus windows.

'I want to say thank you for bringing us here from Cape Town,' he offered. 'My life has just changed; I will never forget this.'

I stared back in amazement, hugged the young fellow and wished him a university education. He turned around and slunk back to the bus, his gold chains swinging slowly from side to side.

'Do you know who that is?' asked a teacher. 'He saw his father shot and killed in front of him last week.'

That brief confrontation made me realise again how many of our primary school children are at risk; how, in Grade 7, big decisions get made. At about this time, many girls begin to experiment with sex and become pregnant or, as the data show clearly, become infected with HIV. At about this time, many boys face important choices about joining gangs with instant money on offer, not to mention drugs.

But this young man, through the help of my friends and colleagues, has joined a special group that, quite possibly, has had a life-changing experience.

Imagine township kids being taught about writing books by none other than the award-winning author Chris van Wyk, who wrote the riveting *Shirley, Goodness and Mercy*. They could not believe their eyes when they met the inspired athletics sensation, Caster Semenya. Their notepads and reflections took them through Freedom Park, the Voortrekker Monument, the Apartheid Museum, the Cradle of Humankind and university campuses. They learnt about finance, history, writing, politics, sport and humanity.

'Some of them have never even been to Cape Town station,' said one of the teachers. Few had been out of the province.

It is difficult not to be moved by their experiences.

Said the principal: 'When we asked them after the tour who would be going to university, every hand shot up.'

I am writing to thank the sponsors and volunteers in the different cities. But, most of all, I want to thank Raquel-Naomi, 8, and Micah-Lael, 2, the children of special friends of mine, who raided their meagre accounts to hand over R500 to the children of Sullivan Primary.

Ordinary people making an extraordinary difference.

Nun so good in a classroom

Bring back old-fashioned discipline

30 September 2009

I have a solution for the education crisis. Flood the schools with nuns. No, really. One of the reasons we had such strong schools, attended by tens of thousands of black students over the past century, was because of church schools, especially schools with nuns.

Many of my friends would complain bitterly about the relentless discipline of the Catholic schools, with those unyielding nuns who had dedicated themselves to the strictest codes of moral and academic behaviour. They got the best academic results, but the alumni detested the sheer discipline. There have been fewer times in our history when that kind of discipline was more sorely needed than now.

Even as a child, I heard amazing stories about schools like Little Flower in Ixopo (of then Natal), where the nuns not only produced the top matriculants in the land, they even wrote some of the textbooks.

True, the students were kept from worldly pleasures and we boys listened with wide eyes to the obviously exaggerated tales about what would happen if a love-starved girl from Immaculata Secondary School in Cape Town got hold of you.

So when the collapse of your country's school system makes it onto the pages of the *New York Times*, you know that it is not only the natives who see the wrecking ball that bashes the majority of our schools every day. The crisis is also seen from afar, and of all the stories the famous paper could report on, the state of South Africa's schools is seen as serious enough to feature on its pages.

And what the *New York Times* reports on has appeared countless times in this column: lazy teachers, irresponsible unions, lack of accountability, and the collapse of discipline. The children are not the problem; it is the adults who have squandered their life chances and put an entire society at risk.

This explains the relative success of Zimbabwe's education system; it was run largely by church schools. True, those same schools produced Robert Gabriel Mugabe, hardly an angel, but nevertheless the routines of learning and the rhythms of discipline were established early on in their school system – a system unfortunately destroyed by the Smith regime through war.

We had our 'Smith' moment in 1954, when Bantu Education was installed as an antidote to the church schools that produced the Tambos and the Mandelas, able men of letters who established legal offices in downtown Johannesburg at a time when it was unheard of for black people to do so.

Perhaps we need to rethink some of the practices of those church schools. School prayers taught gratitude. Bible reading aided basic literacy. Corporal punishment reminded students not only of the sin of the moment, but also of the consequences of disobedience in the hereafter. Yes, the environment was harsh and, no doubt, some scars might remain as painful memories for some.

But at least children learnt values that made for good education and for solid citizens. My friends who complain about their strict ecclesiastical education are all high achievers in the corporate world, in higher education and in public service.

It is clear to me that we have the wrong people teaching our children. Attend any graduation ceremony and watch the students from law, medicine and accounting faculties walk across the stage to get their degrees. They are excited, enthusiastic and full of energy. Then watch the education students traipse across the stage. They are slow-moving and depressed, and lacking in energy and enthusiasm.

We are still not attracting the best and the brightest into teaching. In fact, we are training students who often themselves know only of dysfunctional schools and the lack of discipline in their own experience. Their socialisation is so powerful that one is seldom able to get through what it actually means to teach (sporadically, when you feel like it) in three to four years, after their twelve years of witnessing, as children, the chaos in public schools.

That is why many of my black students ran into problems when we placed them for their practice teaching in some of the better organised, formerly white schools. They were in culture shock, which had nothing to do with race and everything to do with a disciplined routine that required preparing properly and teaching every day.

Instead of recruiting Cuban doctors or Zimbabwean teachers, my advice to President Zuma is to solicit the support of His Holiness, and to rope in nuns from all over the world to teach our children.

Sinking deeper into mediocrity

Adjusting expectations downwards is very dangerous

23 February 2011

I have in front of me the 2010 'Statement of Results' for the National Senior Certificate statement of a youngster who demands to study at university. It reads: Afrikaans 43, English 39, Mathematical Literacy 38, Life Orientation 78, Business Studies 41, Computer Applications Technology 31, Life Sciences 28.

At the bottom of the certificate is this unbelievable statement: 'The candidate qualifies for the National Senior Certificate and fulfils the minimum requirements for admission to higher education.'

Understandably, this young woman takes these words literally, and correctly demands a seat in any place of higher learning. With the young woman's claim to study I have no problem. With society that sets the bar for performance so low, I have serious problems. Slowly but surely we are digging our collective graves in the sinkhole of mediocrity from which we are unlikely to emerge.

We make excellence sound like a 'white' thing. Behind a massive wave of populism, and in the misguided name of *regstelling* (setting right the past), we open access to resources and universities to young people without the hard work necessary to attain those gifts and to succeed once there. Of course, you are a racist if you question this kind of mindlessness; how else do you, as a politician, defend yourself against the critics of mediocrity in an election year?

I miss Steve Biko. In the thinking of black consciousness, he would have railed against the low standards we set for black achievement, in the language of the 1970s.

In her Senior Certificate results, this young (incidentally black) person did not achieve anything above 50 per cent for any exam subject, but we tell her she can proceed to higher studies. What are we saying? That black students are somehow less capable and therefore need these pathetic results to access higher education? No, I am sorry, but today I am angry about the messages we send our children.

I saw black parents and students squirm the other night when I addressed a racially diverse audience and made this point clear: 'If a black student requires from you different treatment and lower academic demands because of an argument about disadvantage, tell them to take a hike.' (Okay, I used stronger language.)

I saw white teachers squirm when I made the other important point: 'If you have lower academic expectations of black children because of what they look like, or where they come from, that is the worst kind of racism.'

Our society, schools and universities have adjusted expectations downwards, especially in relation to black students, and that is dangerous in a country that holds so much promise for excellence.

As stories come rolling in from across the country for our book on great South African teachers, I am struck by one thing. It is that many black professionals who are chartered accountants, medical scientists or corporate lawyers tell of attending ordinary public schools under apartheid, often in rural areas, and having teachers at the time who, despite the desperate poverty and inequality, held high expectations of their learners. There was no compromising on academic standards; there was homework every day; there was punishment for low performance; and there was constant motivation to rise above one's circumstances.

Not so today. Mathematical Literacy, for example, is a cop-out, a way of compensating for poor maths teaching in the mainstream. Parents of Grade 9 children, listen carefully – do not let your school force your child into taking Maths Literacy. If they do, they will struggle to find access to academic degree studies at serious universities. Insist on your child doing Mathematics in Grade 10, for that important choice determines what your child writes in Grade 12.

It is not, of course, mathematical literacy as such that I am concerned about; there are good teachers of the subject. It is about the message we are communicating, namely that children cannot do maths.

In other words, the message is once again that of low expectations. Do not buy into this culture of mediocrity in the way your child makes subject choices. Also, tell him or her not to take Life Orientation too seriously. As you can see in the young woman's results above, there is no positive relationship between high marks in academic subjects and the 'easier' subject of Life Orientation.

Young people with better results than these are still without work. The marketplace and serious universities know this child will not succeed with these kinds of results, even if Umalusi does not 'get it'.

TALK ABOUT UNIVERSITIES

'Professor, I came home and told my family that we must change, that not all white people are bad and that we must respect them.'

Don't kid yourself about BAs

Get a mind-broadening education – and a large pizza

8 December 2010

'So what's the difference between a BA degree and a large pizza?' one of my student leaders recently asked a large group of parents inquiring about sending their child to university. 'A large pizza can feed a family of four,' she joked. I laughed, then cried.

Laughed, because of the obvious wit of the comparison. Cried, because this is one of the most misleading pieces of information about Bachelor of Arts degrees in South Africa today.

It was not that I hadn't overheard 'BA jokes' before. At my previous university, there was rampant talk among female students of a *BA-man-soek* specialisation (meaning 'BA-find-a-husband'). After all, what other reason could one have for doing a BA than to prowl the campus for a life mate?

Sadly, many parents buy into this myth about the uselessness of a BA. The actuarial science degree gets you a specific job, as do degrees in marketing, optometry or accountancy. With this common-sense (though often wrong) understanding of a degree, parents guide their children away from a BA towards 'something more practical', or 'something that can get you a job'.

The truth is I have seen as many BA students getting good jobs as I have seen BComm Accounting students without jobs. In fact, I would argue that a BA from a good university is likelier to get you different kinds of jobs – not a bad option in an economic recession – than a single-career job that comes with a degree in, say, physiotherapy or law.

Why is that? A good BA qualification from a good university would have taught you generic competencies seldom learnt in narrow occupational degrees. A good BA would have given you the foundations of learning across disciplines, such as sociology, psychology, politics, anthropology and languages. A good BA would have given you access to critical thinking skills, appreciation of literature, understanding of cultures, the uses of power, the mysteries of the mind, the organisation of societies, the complexities of leadership, the art of communication and the problem of change. A good BA would have taught you something about the human condition, and so something about yourself. In short, a good BA degree would have given you a solid education that forms the basis for workplace training.

The head of the Johannesburg Stock Exchange, a gentleman called Russell Loubser, taught me a valuable lesson the other day. I was talking to this astute businessman about the training function of universities when he gently chided me – the education man – with timeless wisdom. 'No, professor,' he said, 'you educate them. I train them.'

This is where the American colleges get it right when they talk about a liberal arts education in the undergraduate years. There is more than enough time for the occupational training that comes later and is best done in the workplace.

What we fail to do at South African universities is to educate young minds broadly in ethics, values, reasoning, appreciation, problem solving, argumentation and logic. Locked into single-discipline thinking, our young people fail to learn that the most complex social and human problems cannot be solved except through interdisciplinary thinking that crosses these disciplinary boundaries.

For example, anyone who thought HIV/Aids was simply an immunological problem is a victim of the kind of narrow training restricted to the biomedical sciences. The syndrome is as much a sociological, economic, political and cultural problem as it might be a problem of virology. Don't get me wrong: HIV causes Aids, period. What I am arguing is that its resolution will take more than an injection, and that is the broader value that a BA degree can offer a well-educated youngster.

So, the next time you hear people make jokes about a worthless BA degree, tell them about Bobby Godsell (the BA graduate who served as the CEO of AngloGold Ashanti), Vincent Maphai (the BA graduate who rose to serve as chairman of BHP Billiton), Clem Sunter (the famous scenario planner and former chairman of the Anglo-American Chairman's Fund), Phumzile Mlambo-Ngcuka (the former deputy president of South Africa) or Saki Macozoma (the chairman of Stanlib and Liberty Life).

The list of highly successful graduates with BAs, or equivalent degrees, is endless.

Then go out and buy your family a large pizza.

Travel does a world of good

Studying abroad has a powerful influence on thinking

3 November 2010

The four students waiting for me in the small room looked very different from the typical students I had come to find on any university campus.

Here on our campus in the eastern Free State things are especially tough. Poverty is extreme and the demands on social welfare in the surrounding communities are enormous. Virtually every student on this campus studies with financial aid of various kinds. Many of them were failed by dysfunctional, poor rural schools, but managed to scrape together the money and the willpower to enter university.

So why do these four students look so different? Why are they laughing with such freedom? Why are they so full of energy? What is it that distinguishes these first-years from the rest of the student body?

These students were part of a group of seventy-one first-years who had just returned from a three-week stay at top universities on the east coast of the USA. But beyond the obvious excitement of a short period of studying abroad, I was about to discover something quite dramatic about the life-changing experiences these young people have had.

So I posed the critical question: what was the one thing in your experience abroad that changed you? They all rushed to speak, and what I heard in the next

20 minutes was the most moving account of changed lives I had listened to in a very long time.

The first student jumped ahead of her colleagues and made the startling confession: 'In my community, Professor, I had learnt to despise gays and lesbians. But when I went to New York University, they discussed these issues openly, and I realised how bigoted I was towards people with a different sexual orientation to my own. I am embarrassed about those feelings I used to have about other people.'

I sat in stunned silence. I was really not expecting the feedback to go so deep, to be so honest and so personal.

The next student butted in, and this time I almost fell from my chair.

'Professor, I came home and told my family that we must change, that not all white people are bad and that we must respect them.'

No student I know of will willingly and openly make these kinds of disclosures, especially in our race-sensitive, race-obsessed society. This student in the harsh environment of a poor, rural area could easily have carried her racial grievance on her sleeve, but she had been changed in a remarkable way.

She told how her white home-stay parents in the United States treated her as their own daughter; how they did everything to make this young woman from the Free State university feel loved and cared for; and how they cried the day she had to return to South Africa. This experience of living with, and being loved by a white family, forever changed the young student's view of white people in her own country.

The third student was overheating as he waited to tell his story.

'I thought the only way to raise your problems and concerns was to fight, to demand things and to struggle. But I saw that the students there spend their time thinking, arguing and making their case with reason and with logic.'

I smiled inwardly, wondering how this student would be received in a national culture that believes in destroying and breaking down rather than in making powerful arguments. Imagine how university cultures would change if there were tens of thousands of students like this young man.

I am convinced that one of the main reasons why we have so many problems on our campuses is that our students are ignorant of any other model for behaviour than what they see among their peers. Racism, homophobia and the desire to destroy come from what they observe around them in their native land. What they see becomes the new 'normal', and we all suffer.

What changed these students was that they were taken out of their isolation in central South Africa. They saw other norms and values that govern student and community behaviour. They realised for the first time there is a better way to be human, to be a citizen, to be a student. And the impact of three weeks of study abroad on seventy-one student leaders cannot be calculated in rands and cents.

I know this is too expensive, but the ideal would be for all South African students to be placed in top universities in other countries. It would change the often narrow-minded, conservative and self-destructive behaviour of South African youth. It would challenge a value system in education that is in serious decay.

Race holds us back after class

Should race determine admission to university?

9 September 2010

A firestorm has broken out at the University of Cape Town over the question as to whether race should be used to determine admission to university studies.

In the case of its medical school, UCT not only calculates different admissions criteria for white and black students; it further determines differential pass rates for Indian students versus coloured students versus African students.

The vice-chancellor, Dr Max Price, is adamant that this is the best available methodology for racial redress at UCT. His fiercest critic, Dr Neville Alexander, argues exactly the opposite – that race labels do more harm than good in a post-apartheid democracy. The irony of the two positions is in itself intriguing: a white man defending racial redress, a black man criticising it.

The question, of course, is not about racial redress. All our institutions, and especially UCT, need to repair the damage done in the past, not only as far as the racial demography of its student body is concerned, but especially in terms of staffing equity.

In years past, UCT has been more likely to hire an academic from England, to which the academic umbilical cord still remains firmly attached, than it was likely to hire a top black professor from South Africa. The university acknowledged as much in its public apology to the brilliant scholar, Professor Archie Mafeje, for not appointing him despite having more than one opportunity to do so.

The central question in the UCT debacle is whether we can correct apartheid's wrongs by invoking the very racial categories that had offended and divided us in the past. I cannot think of anything more bizarre, for the manner in which UCT approaches the question of redress is the best way of keeping apartheid thinking alive and well in the consciousness of most South Africans.

As critics of UCT's policy correctly assert, using race to determine admission is meaningless in the suburban economy of that institution, where the top academic schools have enrolled more and more black students of all stripes over the past two decades. This means that black children at schools such as Bishops, Westerford or SACS are less likely to be first-generation university students than was the case ten or more years ago.

These children are not disadvantaged, at least not educationally or materially; in fact, more and more of these black students appear in the top 10 per cent of their class and assume leadership positions in their schools. To advantage such students in entrance to economics or medicine studies at UCT is laughable.

Some deep thinkers would claim that disadvantage is more than the school one attends or the amount of money in one's home. Disadvantage is also psychological – those barriers to confidence that remain long after material differences have been resolved between white and black.

Frankly, I find this to be a shaky argument when it comes to the middle classes of whatever colour.

All young people struggle with confidence – poor children more so than those from well-resourced families. All young people find the adjustment to university difficult, especially those with less money. Black children from well-to-do homes do as well as white children whose families are similarly well-off. So, what is the problem?

The problem is class, not race. There is a much greater disparity (in terms of resources, confidence and university preparation) between black students from Khayelitsha and Manenberg in the Cape, than between a white or a black student from Wynberg Boys or Girls High School.

Where you have studied matters; where you live matters; whether your parents have a job, or whether there are computers and books in your home matters. The student's degree of pigmentation is, to be honest, irrelevant.

Of course, what intellectuals like Neville Alexander realise is that retaining those ridiculous four racial categories is a prescriptive act; it not only selects students for studies at one of South Africa's most prestigious universities, it also instils in the minds of young people ways of thinking about themselves and others.

Race categories order the world for students in the same way it did for their parents before the 1990s. This is the great danger facing social transformation in South Africa.

When my student leaders at the University of the Free State came to see me recently, they asked that we do away with racial specifications in the choice of the HKs (*huiskomitees*) or residence committees.

As one who grew up in the old apartheid system, I was reluctant, for students tend to choose leaders who look like them. That has happened in some cases, but there are more good news stories: Emily Hobhouse residence chose its first black 'prime' in its history a few weeks ago. We should listen to our young people.

Don't look back in anger

Building resilience to move past anger

11 August 2010

I was having an early morning 'rector's breakfast' in my office last week with some of my students from the university.

It was the kind of interaction with students that every university principal dreams of. Black and white, male and female, first-years and seniors. They were laughing and high-fiving, all the time bombarding me with questions of various kinds – personal, political and professional.

This warm, enjoyable breakfast was light years away from what would happen later that day when a few angry students (fewer than a hundred out of thirty thousand students) disrupted the first few games of the annual intervarsity with our neighbours from the North-West University.

Towards the end of the breakfast one of the senior students present, a smart black fellow who spent much of his time in one of the residences, nervously posed this question: 'Professor,' he asked, 'how do I move on from my state of anger? How did you deal with your anger? How, please tell me, can I move on?'

The room suddenly went quiet. I could sense the lump-in-the-throat feeling among us. This young man was courageous, and we were all unprepared for his question.

There is a lot of anger going around among segments of black students on South African campuses. One of the big mistakes we often make is to dismiss this anger even before trying to understand it. It is only in understanding black student anger that we are able as education leaders to resolve the sources of such discontent.

There are, of course, different kinds of anger in the black student community. There is the anger of the township *skollie*, the uncouth thug who should never be admitted to a place of higher learning.

There is the anger of the political opportunist, the student connected to outside political parties, whose only goal in life is to make the leap from university campus to party deployment in the shortest time possible. This kind of anger hijacks the noble language of anti-apartheid struggles from yesteryear, masking acts of tyranny and destruction in the democratic present.

But there is another type of anger that we need to understand and appreciate, and that is the anger of the young man at the rector's breakfast.

A black student at a historically white university (whether it is Wits University or the University of Pretoria) would often complain of small acts of aggression, marginalisation and sometimes straightforward abuse. He sits in a residence meeting where people speak only Afrikaans, and he does not understand a thing.

A drunk, white student once called him a 'kaffir' in the corridor of his residence. He struggles to find money to take a taxi to campus from his township. There are some days on which he goes hungry. He looks around him and sees symbols and ceremonies that he cannot relate to. Some lecturers might even ignore him when he raises his hand in class, or remind him repeatedly that few students pass the course he is taking. And he remembers the ugliness of initiation from his first-year experience.

Slowly, slowly these little and big things build up a resentment in that student so that he later makes no distinction between direct forms of abuse (like being sworn at) and his general hardships as a student. By the time he becomes a senior, this student is combustible.

I have lots of time for this kind of student because, a long time ago, I had some of these experiences myself as an undergraduate student. We need to be responsive to the needs of this student – left unaided, he could do damage to himself and to others.

The discussion that followed at breakfast was supportive. We spoke about learning to be tough, about resilience, and about the fact that all students pass through hardships of various kinds, and that growing up and growing strong were an important part of university learning.

We talked about owning the space around you, of not seeing a public university as belonging to one group or another, but as belonging to all of us. We talked about confronting bad behaviour in constructive ways.

I pointed out that a sign of maturity is to see the abuser as the victim, the one who needs help, rather than to have the abuser determine how you feel about yourself. In the memorable words of Eleanor Roosevelt, 'No one can make you feel inferior without your permission.'

As the students left, each one being hugged as they passed through the door, I saw many smiles on their faces. But the smile on the face of the angry black student was priceless.

How 'journalism' sets us back

Sensationalism destroys a fragile future

9 June 2010

As the experienced television personality Debora Patta rounded in on the young, white Afrikaans-speaking student leader, it was clear she was not interested in information; she was intent on humiliation.

The young woman represented a conservative political body with an on-campus branch, the Freedom Front Plus. The student was defending her right to represent the interests of Afrikaners on campus.

She acknowledged the mistakes made by her forbears, but she also described the struggle more than 100 years ago against English penetration of the country.

She does not want to be apologetic about the past, said the student, but she is proud to represent Afrikaner interests.

This is too much for Patta: 'You are a racist,' she provokes without any warning, and tears start streaming down the face of the young woman student.

The imagery was powerful. Patta stands with the microphone, firing questions at the young woman. Behind Patta stands a small crowd of black students. The white student stands, literally and figuratively, with her back against the wall.

Patta interrupts and insults the student with attack-dog tactics, no doubt conscious that the young woman is struggling to answer in English. In less than five minutes Patta breaks down one year of hard, hard work trying to bring together black and white students and staff on a campus that has made huge strides in its attempts to forge reconciliation and social justice in the University of the Free State.

This e.tv show was actually produced and broadcast in 2009. But the story about 'two Free State students' attacking a black high school student was simply too sensational for Patta and other journalists hell-bent on framing the Free State as a racist institution.

If they had done their homework, and not yielded to their lust for racist stories, Patta would have discovered that neither one of the young men alleged to have committed the crime was a student of the University of the Free State at the time of the incident.

In fact, one was never a student and the other had left to study at a neighbouring institution. The charges were narrowed down and it is unclear which of the young men did, in fact, do what the victim claims; the courts will decide.

But why bother with the facts when such a juicy story comes from the Free State and, by implication, the University of the Free State? So, off goes Patta and dusts off a 2009 video to make it part of a 2010 story implicating the university with Reitz images freely available to tarnish the institution (not two young men in an off-campus incident) unfairly once again.

I have no truck with the Freedom Front Plus or for conservative politics generally; yet I also know that a number of white students choose such a party affiliation simply because no other organisation on our political landscape speaks for the interests of conservative students.

In the past year, we acted strongly as a university against racist and sexist incidents on campus. We also put hundreds of hours of training and support into student development in order to bring young people to a sense of their common humanity.

The degree of racial integration in residences of the University of the Free State is much higher than in any other South African institution at the moment. Black and white students have made enormous progress in race relations as they live, travel, study, camp at and invade my home on weekends offering incredible stories of interracial friendship and solidarity.

Individual students have left the University of the Free State for institutions that they believe still offer white-exclusive residences in South Africa, but we have increasingly attracted high-quality white and black students who want to make a difference in the country.

This is what makes the rebroadcasting of Patta's attack on a white student so tragic; it breaks down what our people are trying to build up. It misrepresents in timing and content how the majority of students actually feel.

Sure, both to the left and right, on the margins of this and any other university, you can readily find people for whom racial politics offers a platform for bitterness and a route into off-campus politics.

But most of our thirty thousand students are decent human beings struggling with their inherited stories of the past, and are determined to make the campus and the country a better place for all.

There is a thin line between strong, investigative journalism, and outright prejudice and harassment. What Patta did was cross this line and, in the process, not only destroyed a young woman's confidence, but wrecked fragile race relations on a university campus.

Catch 'em young, send 'em up

Want to curb the university drop-out rate?
Think differently

19 May 2010

There is a solution to the damaging loss of money and talent that comes with tens of thousands of South African students dropping out of university.

Universities lose funding resources; parents lose out on hard-earned savings invested in their children; students lose confidence in their ability to gain a university education; and the country fails to gain another skilled graduate from university.

All round, the consequences of failure and drop-out are devastating for students, families, universities and the country. Until now, few universities have come up with imaginative solutions to the old problem of high drop-out rates.

Here's a brilliant idea proposed by a friend: send high school students to university before they finish high school.

What?

Tshepo is a Grade 10 student at, say, JB Mkhize High in a rural township school. Nobody in his family has ever gone to university. Tshepo is very smart and longs to go beyond Grade 12 to study further and get a decent job.

Despite the fact that Tshepo finds himself in a school with a 30 per cent pass rate in the senior certificate examination, he passes all his subjects and finds himself among the top 5 per cent of learners in his school.

Because of his natural talent and personal efforts, Tshepo will pass Grade 12, but the gap between a poor school education and demanding university training will be too much for the young man. He is destined to drop out.

So the university goes to Tshepo and offers him the option of going to university every Saturday morning from 09:00 to 15:00 where he can do either Psychology I, Chemistry I or Accountancy I over a three-year period – during his senior high school years.

Tshepo jumps at the opportunity and gains the one thing that first-generation university students desperately need – university knowledge.

He learns how to take summary notes in large classes.

He learns to use the computer as a tool for learning.

He learns to find his way through a university library, using online resources as well as sources on the shelves.

He learns to work on complex problems in psychology or accounting in groups of talented, but equally disadvantaged, students from other schools.

He learns to consult with tutors and professors.

He learns to find his way around the campus buildings.

And he learns to find his own voice in classrooms, laboratories and seminars.

In other words, when Tshepo reaches university in three years' time, he has already been there. This is the crucial difference between Tshepo and first-year students who come in cold – he already has the critical knowledge generally needed for success at a university.

Of course, he will learn disciplinary knowledge in one of the three subject areas over many Saturday classes, but what he also gains are the skills and confidence to negotiate his way through university life, which can be a frightening experience.

The arguments against this innovative thinking to address the problem of high drop-out rates are predictable. For example, there will be those who ask: what about the scaffolding knowledge that Tshepo needs to do well in a first-year university course?

Well, many university courses, such as psychology, are not dependent on what one knows from school. In addition, since school knowledge in fields such as accountancy is often weakly learnt and weakly linked to university-level accountancy, the bridging knowledge can be built into the design of the first-year curriculum.

Of course, this kind of innovation demands the best university teachers and an intensive model of academic support. A strong mentorship programme is critical, and open, regular feedback is important to guide Tshepo over the three-year period. But once these foundations have been laid, Tshepo would have the competence and confidence to deal with the rigours of university life, including lousy university teachers ...

Here's the brilliance of this model: should Tshepo pass one of these three courses while at high school, which I have no doubt he will, he can gain the credits for the course once he registers at the university offering this plan. In other words, Tshepo would not have to pay a cent for the course and, in addition, he would have a lighter first-year load than other students.

But the benefits run downwards as well: Tshepo will now probably do much better in the Grade 12 examinations because of the skills and confidence gained through his university-level course over three years.

Is it the journey that matters?

Impossible choices, how would you decide?

5 May 2010

It's that time of the year again. Grade 12 students with families in tow flock to universities around the country to help them decide where and what to study.

Open Day, as it's called, can be nerve-wracking for students. There are so many options, so much pressure, and the decision could alter one's life forever.

What if you choose something you discover too late you do not like at all? We've all been there, of course, and it does not help telling a prospective university student that most first-year students do not make up their minds until they arrive on campus to study.

Nothing distresses me more than the white parent who wants his or her child to become a doctor, but suspects that the seven faculties in the country that offer the medical degree (MBChB) actually discriminate against white students as such.

Years ago it was quite simple: one simply took the students with the best matriculation marks and gave them access to medical school. I certainly remember when I was at high school that newspaper interviews with the so-called top ten in my neighbourhood had each one of them mouthing medicine at UCT or Stellenbosch. Given the unhappy state of unequal schooling, it was not surprising, therefore, that white students completely dominated medical school intakes, with the exception of one school established, in apartheid's crazy logic, for blacks at the University of Natal.

Now fast forward to 2009/2010.

Susanna le Roux (not her real name) achieved a clean deck of seven distinctions in the 2009 senior certificate examination at her formerly white school. She worked hard all through high school, often sleeping only four hours a night because of her determination to do well in her school exams. She sacrificed many school outings and family holidays to achieve her goal. And Susanna had only one goal in mind, and that was to be a doctor. She was the top matric student in her school and in her district, and third overall in her province.

'Susanna,' says her teacher, 'was not one of those children who simply showed up for her exams and passed. She had to work hard for her distinctions.' Imagine the joy of her family, teachers and peers when Susanna did so well. Then came the shock: Susanna applied to medical school at a well-known university and was informed in a polite letter that her application had been unsuccessful.

Molly Radebe (not her real name) achieved one A, two Bs and three Cs in the 2009 senior certificate examination. In her poor township these were the best matric results in the forty-year history of the school. Molly was a hero.

The school did not have a science laboratory, but Molly got a B in natural sciences. The mathematics teacher only had a college diploma in mathematics and was often absent from school (there were nasty rumours that he was also managing a taxi rank), yet Molly worked hard to achieve a B in mathematics. She did not miss an opportunity to tell her friends she did 'real maths', not the watered-down maths literacy that all the other matriculants took.

But, most of all, Molly was proud of her A in English, for even though her home languages were Zulu and Sepedi (her father and mother's languages, respectively), Molly was determined to do well in English.

She even walked 7 km after school, every day for two years, to take extra English classes from a retired teacher in one of the white suburbs. Molly applied to the same medical school as Susanna; she, however, received a warm letter of congratulations announcing that she had been awarded a place in medical school for 2010.

The medical school in question had built into its admission requirements a factor that sought to level the playing field for students such as Molly and Susanna. It was not only interested in the raw scores from the matriculation examination, but also in students' potential to do well.

In the reasoning of the School of Medicine, Susanna would have had good teachers, predictable teaching time-tables, the Internet at home, parents who had studied at university themselves and who could therefore help and advise the young white girl in her choices.

Molly, on the other hand, would have studied by candlelight in a school without good teachers and a poor culture of teaching and learning. She was a first-generation university student and had to figure out the complexities of the medical school application forms all by herself. For her to overcome all the obstacles to achieving success in matric makes Molly an ideal candidate for medical school.

Did the medical school in question make the right decision?

Young lives hang in the balance

Can university compensate for twelve years of bad schooling?

20 January 2010

I need your advice. Two young black women came to my office last week to request financial assistance for their first year of studies at the University of the Free State.

They are desperately poor and, on paper, their exam results are not good. They both passed the 2009 senior certificate examination, but they both failed one or two subjects by a percentage point. They therefore missed the pass mark required to gain access to the government's financial aid scheme, and their parents are either unemployed or domestic workers.

Here's my question: should the university find the money to give these two young people a chance at higher education?

Are we, on the one hand, setting them up for failure in the academically demanding environment of a university? Or, on the other hand, are we condemning these two vulnerable young women to a life of unemployment and desperation?

As is so often the case, I was really torn between these questions and decided to ask the two students to write me a letter explaining why they should be given a chance to study at university. I wanted to know who they were, where they came from and, of course, whether they could write competently and persuasively. Maybe, just maybe, their writing could help us make what, for them, could be a life-altering decision.

A day later, the two letters arrived. They were inspiring and disturbing at the same time. The very fact that these two young women had survived poverty, violence and a miserable school education is astonishing. They walked 23 km to school every day. One of them has a father who is violent at home, who drowns himself in alcohol and who was sent to prison, leaving his destitute family out on the street. The other has a large family, supported on a domestic worker's salary. They would arrive home at night after taking the long walk from school and simply drop off to sleep.

But the two girls, good friends, persisted. They took part in school events, such as debating societies and poetry competitions. They became student leaders in their schools. They won competitions that brought computers to their impoverished schools. Whereas most teenagers would have dropped out into the seductions of easy living on the streets, these two girls had showed uncommon resilience.

'I only have one dream,' said the letter from one of the young women, 'and that is to take my family out of slavery.'

These students were lucky in another respect. They were identified by a middle-aged white woman who encouraged them with her own meagre resources. Now, as they stood in my office, the teary-eyed white woman and the wide-eyed black students, I had to make a decision.

We could, of course, look at the senior certificate re-sults and make a snap decision. Or we could reason as fol-lows: these girls, placed in one of the fancy schools around South Africa, would no doubt have produced As and Bs in their subjects. But poverty and history had placed them in terrible environments, including under-resourced schools.

The fact that they had survived these tragedies sug-gests that they are tough; that they realise that the stakes are very high; and that failure is not an option. These girls have the potential to do extremely well. After all, they never missed classes at school and even stretched themselves to take part in extramural activities.

Unlike some of my well-off students, these two women will take nothing for granted. There is every indication that, with the right support, they will succeed, because what had failed them in the past was the school system.

But is this realistic? Can the university compensate for twelve years of bad schooling and hard living? Is ours a progressive pipe dream that could further shatter already vulnerable lives?

How should we decide?

Another future in our hands

Desperate to break the cycle of poverty

27 January 2010

I am sorry to do this to you again, but I need further advice. The other day a young white student and her mother showed up at my door.

The daughter had passed her senior certificate examination with moderate results, barely failing in one subject. Her marks were good enough to qualify her to study for a bachelor's degree.

My initial inclination was to deny the student access; after all, I had announced that we planned to raise the academic admission standards and take only the best black and white students into the university.

The problem is her compelling story. She comes from a broken home. Raised for the most part by a single mother who is unemployed, this young woman is desperate to break the cycle of poverty in her family.

She wants to become a teacher, but was told that government bursaries on offer are for black students. Now, as her mother looks at me, I see in her that familiar, desperate plea that conveys a simple but powerful message: 'Please take my daughter into the university. This is our last chance; we need a break.'

There are different ways of looking at this problem.

On the one hand, there are strong arguments for available places for academically average students to be reserved for students from disadvantaged schools. The reasoning is that academic performance reflects the poverty of the schooling, and that students who pass reasonably well despite such conditions deserve funding and placement.

Here is a white student. Her parents were advantaged under apartheid. She had access to a solid education in a white, well-resourced school.

Despite this, she manages to achieve only an average performance for her senior certificate. She therefore cannot demand resources and placement unless she has superior results, like three or more A symbols.

A racially harsh version of this line of reasoning I once heard in a horrible twist on that *New York, New York* song in reference to white South Africans: 'If they can't make it here, they can't make it anywhere.'

On the other hand, this is a South African student living in poverty. It is wrong, some would say, to make a judgment for or against university admission based on race.

After all, apartheid was not simply a system of racial discrimination; it was also a capitalist system that ensured that a white underclass existed alongside a white middle class, even during the high point of racial laws and policies. It is disingenuous, therefore, to dismiss the claims of the white student on the grounds of race alone.

Furthermore, what did this child have to do with apartheid? Must she now be punished for the sins of the fathers? It's not her fault that she was born with a white skin, and she did not perpetrate the terrible laws that oppressed black people. And who knows what kinds of struggles she had to survive in her domestic situation as her mother battled day after day to keep her in school?

Moreover, how do we build a non-racial democracy if we constantly make decisions, even among the common poor, on the basis of race?

I asked the mother and her daughter to leave all their documents with me so that I could consult my colleagues and think about this conundrum. That, in short, is the case study.

How would you advise me to proceed?

In closing, many of you must be wondering what happened to the two black students who came to see me. We have decided to admit them to university based on their potential. We have found the money for their studies.

But they are required to meet me, as their mentor, once every fortnight for an hour each. During this time they will learn to read and analyse complex texts, perform advanced computer functions, write deeply thoughtful essays, and debate with me on some major issues in and around their disciplines.

Let me thank those readers who promised to add to the funding for these two young women's studies. Thank you all.

Varsities in fight for standards

Resist the pressure to lower standards at all costs

9 December 2009

Our universities are at a crossroads. There is enormous pressure on them to open their doors to all students. That is correct: a university must, and should, be accessible to all students irrespective of their race, class, gender, disability or national origins.

It is the one institution that economists of higher education will tell you can level the playing field in terms of economic inequalities between classes.

A degree matters much more than a high school qualification in terms of future income and, in tightly-knit domestic structures, as found in South Africa, a degree will more often than not make a marked difference in the welfare of the family unit. The stakes are high.

Every year, my office is besieged by students and their families, desperate for their children to complete their studies and obtain a degree. This year seemed worse, as the recession affected both poor and middle-class families.

In all universities in South Africa, large amounts of money are set aside to enable needy students to gain the knowledge that makes a social and economic difference in society. That this money is not always efficiently spent constitutes a separate discussion.

The major problem is that there are not enough students with the academic foundations necessary to obtain and retain scholarship funding. But I can safely say that I know of no university that would turn away an academically strong student on the grounds of a lack of funding.

The problem is that more and more students are entering university completely unprepared for the demands of higher education. That much we already knew.

In response, universities have developed sophisticated programmes to bridge the gap between school under-preparedness and the demands of higher education. Some enjoy modest to high levels of success, but for many students these programmes provide little benefit.

And here is where the problem lies, for at this point a university can do one of two things.

It can lower the standards demanded for success in a course or programme, and artificially inflate the academic results of weak students. In this way, the university has solved the ubiquitous 'throughput' problem – it keeps the students happy; it relieves itself of public scrutiny and political pressure; the student retains the funding and picks up a degree at the end of three or more years.

A university can, however, do what is right. It could set high standards for academic performance for all students. It could select students based on measures of potential (not only Grade 12 results) and invest heavily in those it admits to ensure that they are able not only to meet, but also to exceed, the standards of performance required for the degree.

When students fail despite intense academic support, such a university then takes the hard decision not to allow the student to continue his or her studies. Such universities worry about the integrity of an academic degree, and the danger of delivering doctors or teachers without the knowledge and skills required for such critical jobs.

This is where the politics begins, as I am reminded year after year. The student refuses to accept this academic decision. The race card is pulled with alarming frequency, especially at formerly white universities – poor results must be because the institution and its professors are racist; there can be no other explanation.

The access card is played at black universities: 'I must be able to study, irrespective of my performance,' some students tell me. 'Education should be free and open to all, and so what if I miss half of my classes?' a student recently asked me. My jaw dropped.

Because the stakes are so high, students resort to all kinds of measures. Cheating in examinations is one; writing to senior politicians, even premiers and cabinet ministers, is another. Outright threats are not uncommon. Charges of racism and 'the lack of transformation' (whatever that means) are familiar sticks with which to beat university managers.

Make no mistake, our universities are under huge pressure to lower standards and inflate results. When institutions of higher learning succumb to such pressure, we all lose – especially talented poor students.

Something has got to give

A case of institutional complicity

21 October 2009

As is the case with all South African universities, the history of the University of the Free State is not unblemished.

About a hundred metres to the left of where I stand is the famous Bram Fischer residence (affectionately called *Vishuis*), named after the father of the younger Fischer. This century-old student residence is living testimony to the proud history of the Free State university.

About a hundred metres directly behind me is the Reitz student residence, a place of infamy that brought great shame to our university and unprecedented outrage to our country when the world saw four young white men racially humiliate five black workers.

In the past few months I have visited the grounds of Reitz, often in an attempt to understand how such an atrocity could have been committed on the grounds of an institution of higher learning.

I believe I now have part of the answer, and that answer has important implications for how we move towards healing, forgiveness and social justice on our campus and in our country.

The biggest mistake to make in analysing the Reitz incident is to explain it in terms of individual pathology.

But to dismiss the video simply as a product of four bad apples is too easy an explanation. This video recording was preceded by a long series of protests against racial integration, especially in the university's residences.

Not all of these racially charged incidents made it into the press. In fact, were it not for the public release of the video recording, no one outside the university would have known about them. And few outside the campus realise that what is now regarded as an offensive video won a residence award for its content.

The question facing us, therefore, is a disturbing one, and it is this: what is it within the institution that has made it possible for such an atrocity to be committed?

And there are other questions. Why is it that, one after another, parents and colleagues have told me that the incident was, and I quote, 'blown out of all proportion'?

Why is it that so many adults came to tell me – as if it mattered – that Oros cold drink was used to simulate the boys urinating onto food?

What must I make of the many representations to my office to inform me that the boys (I quote again) 'loved the *squeezas* and brought them food from their parents' farms'?

When the focus of analysis shifts from that of individual pathology to one of institutional culture, it becomes clear that the Reitz problem is not simply about four racially troubled students. It is, without question, also a problem of institutional complicity.

For this reason, it is clear that the deeper issues of racism and bigotry that prompt conflict at our university –

and at many others – will not be resolved in the courts. Whoever wins or loses in the Reitz case, the social, cultural and ideological complexities that stand in the way of transformation will remain, and I will have to deal with them – unless we do something differently.

The case in a criminal court will go ahead, as will that before the Equality Court; and I can have no influence on the deliberations.

The question we all have to deal with is this: what kind of country do we want to build?

Me first, and then maybe you

We forget that it's all about people

16 September 2009

It was an unusual request. The mother of a student was about to die. The intravenous feeding had been stopped and the end was near.

Would the mother survive long enough to witness her daughter's graduation later that week? Would the university consider taking the graduation ceremony to the student's house so that her weak mother could witness this special event before she departed?

The bureaucratic answer, of course, was 'no'. There are certain rules and procedures for graduation. Scores of people have special roles to play in taking each student through the various processes that lead to the award of the degree on graduation day. And, of course, it had never been done before and could set a dangerous precedent for future students with similar requests.

To the credit of my colleagues, the immediate answer was 'yes'. And so the entire entourage moved to the simple home on the outskirts of Bloemfontein.

There, sitting upright with a courageous face was the dying mother. On the couch next to her sat the beaming daughter surrounded by family members.

We donned the bright, heavy gowns. We marched the short distance from one room to the next. We constituted the meeting per the rules. We read the Scriptures and prayed. We read the citation for the degree. The student walked two steps towards the small bench to kneel as she was capped.

She rose to applause from the small gathering and walked towards the smiling mother. As they hugged in joy, the tears flowed freely around the room.

So much of what is wrong in our schools and in our society is that we forget a simple principle of service delivery: it is about people.

So often at a table in a restaurant or in a long queue at Home Affairs those serving us are more obsessed with the rules and regulations that order the menu or control traffic flow that we forget it is about people. How often have we not heard of a bleeding patient in the emergency room having been told to wait in turn while the nurse drags her feet, only for that patient to die while waiting for service?

We forget, so often, that it is about people.

'People first' (*Batho pele*) is one of those meaningless slogans that you no longer hear simply because the phrase has lost all credibility. We now know it is about me first, my family, my children and my future. Once I have taken care of myself, I might consider your needs. We have sunken into an unbelievably selfish and self-centred society in which the rules apply to you, though not necessarily to me.

This is one of the legacies of our overcontrolled society – it is rule based, even when those rules undermine the honour and dignity of people. It is, also, a consequence of a school system that requires rule-bound logic to resolve problems.

How often have I not heard parents complain about teachers who frown on learners who solve a problem in fewer steps than the textbook requires? Out-of-the-box thinking can limit your career fortunes and damn your educational achievements. It can also do immeasurable harm to innocent people.

Nothing is more uplifting to human beings than when rules are interpreted in ways that lend dignity and respect to other human beings. I was told over and over again by the mother, the grandfather and other relatives of the graduating student that the esteem of the university and its leaders had grown immeasurably by this simple act of generosity.

The goodwill won for the institution cannot be counted in rands and cents. And I am sure that it did not go unnoticed that the black leadership in the graduation ceremony bowed to serve a white student and her family after hours and against the rules.

Just imagine such simple acts of humanity throughout our country becoming known more widely across the boundaries of race, class and national origins. Transformation might just stop being such a dirty word.

TALK ABOUT LEADERSHIP

'... there can be no social change
without personal change.'

You ran a good race, Bra Si

A great man, whom you raised, has taken the baton

24 November 2010

Bra Si, it's been a long time since I attended a township funeral.

Mistake number one was to budget two hours for the event, excluding travel time. Big mistake. I was forced to cancel appointments using the text facility of my cellphone in response to desperate SMS messages from my secretary.

We were into the third hour of the memorial service and the seemingly endless list of speakers was only warming up. It was not simply the apparent lack of concern about time that was fascinating; it was the sheer quality of the entertainment (I hope this word is not disrespectful) that captured my attention.

You realise that a new title has settled firmly into the South African lexicon: 'programme director'. I do not know when this shift of terminology happened, but some suburban colleagues who still insist on 'master of ceremonies' must be culturally tone-deaf.

Our programme director made a clear distinction between the church part, where the gowned ministers did their blessings for a few minutes, and what he called the 'celebration' that followed. Why on earth so many people had to speak remains a mystery to me, but each was determined to have his or her say.

There was the man who played soccer with Bra Si Mokhele; there was the gracious old woman who was his neighbour; there were at least two church subgroups of which Bra Si was a member; there were the two beautiful grandchildren who read a poem; and on and on. Not only the ANC veterans had to have a speaker, but also the ANC itself, whose speaker mercifully did not show up, given the long list of tribute bearers.

A short, plucky man came to the front to inform us that Bra Si had started Bloemfontein Celtic, an institution in these parts. Another man was his golfing partner. Sports buddies of *Oom* Si treated us to actual 'moves', whether it was the dribbling of an imaginary ball or the swing of an imaginary golf club. The audience swung between polite laughter and roars of delight as speaker after speaker honoured Bra Si with moving and hilarious anecdotes.

To get to St Patrick's Church in Mangaung you have to negotiate streets with huge potholes filled with rainwater. You drive past dilapidated homes with broken fences, long neglected by those in authority. In these parts, regular people struggle to make a decent living. And yet here in a large but simple church, I was about to witness one of the ordinary miracles that we so often miss. That miracle was Bra Si.

Here was a man whose compelling story could easily be assembled from the many testimonies of his life as a father, husband, activist, churchgoer and sportsman. He stood up to apartheid by spiriting activists, some now in government, across the borders of the country. He raised his family with stern values and unwavering discipline, but like many of his generation, he would mellow later. He insisted on neat dress; no button undone, no shirt unironed.

His family values inspired a generation, clearly evident at the memorial service as his only wife of many years sat mourning alongside well-disciplined children and grandchildren.

It was Bra Si's generation who decided that despite, or perhaps because of, apartheid they would raise their families and build their communities on the values of respect, self-discipline and learning.

All of this made perfect sense when the man whom he raised, the distinguished science leader, microbiologist and humanitarian came forward to present his tribute to Bra Si. The first president of the National Research Foundation, a man honoured by French presidents and a scholar-leader who had received no less than nine honorary doctorates was the product of an upbringing by Bra Si and his wife.

The next evening this great man, Dr Khotso Mokhele, would be installed as the Chancellor of the University of the Free State. Bra Si missed the great day, to which he had so looked forward, by hours. But what the deceased had delivered over a lifetime was another Bra Si who was now in a position to transfer those core values to another generation of university students.

Go well, Bra Si. In the words of the great man whom you raised: you have fought the good fight, you have finished the race. We take the baton from you and promise to continue to run this daunting race of life in your beloved South Africa.

Arch: Always thinking ahead

Forgiveness is not for sissies

18 August 2010

For a Nobel Laureate who could easily command millions in any currency, this is not where I expect to find the offices of Desmond Mpilo Tutu.

For those of us who grew up in the Cape, Milnerton was the poor white area. Driving down the long stretch of road that shares a name with the nuclear power station, Koeberg, the sight of decaying old buildings become familiar from childhood. If you look carefully, any number of drug dealers and hobos can be seen lying in wait along the side streets, offering an array of illegal wares, especially as dark settles. Aunties in rollers, with red faces that hint at a life of alcohol, hang over the fences.

The directions from the intimidating (at least on the telephone) personal assistant of the Arch are as clear as she is: turn right and left at the Caltex garage opposite the cheapest hotel in the country, the Formula One. This must be a mistake. Half of the grey, warehouse-type buildings are vacated. Why on earth would the Arch settle here? Just across the bay lies the rich land of the Waterfront and any number of classy suites in the shadow of the mountain. 'He surely has choices,' I mutter to my capitalist self.

Up the stairs to the nondescript offices and into the modest waiting room. None of his numerous honorary degrees hangs from the walls, the way doctors decorate their surgeries to remind you they qualified somewhere. And then the wait. This is the first time; I am nervous, a rare reaction to meeting people. Suddenly, there's a loud but warm Afrikaans greeting behind my back – it is the Arch. The Afrikaans catches me off-guard and I stumble with my words.

Into the sparse office of the Arch. He speaks first. 'Let's pray.'

I feel calm after the intercession and the time flies as we discuss flammable topics: the church and politics; education and transformation. I feel an enormous respect for this humble man, remembering how he stood virtually alone as the moral voice of the struggle, while our leaders languished in prison or in exile. He took so many risks that could have ended his life, like diving into the middle of an angry crowd to save a young man from a certain necklacing. He did the same for me in late October 2009, wading into angry political waters to make the bold claim that 'forgiveness is not for sissies'.

We remember what is perhaps his single most important contribution, and that was to send hundreds of black South Africans to get their degrees at American universities in the 1980s.

The Arch had the good sense to know what many of us at the time thought impossible, namely that the apartheid government would have to give up (or, at the very least, share) its power. A new generation of civil servants, academics, entrepreneurs, engineers and architects had to be prepared to take their position in a democratic country one day.

The Arch not only forced American companies to disinvest their resources from upholding the old South African government, he got them to invest in the future preparation of skilled young people to lead in the new country. I was privileged to be one of the beneficiaries of that programme, called the Educational Opportunities Council.

'God has a sense of humour,' he reminds me. With this cue I tell the Arch that I live on Whites Road in Bloemfontein. I worry that he is going to choke the way he laughs about a black man living on Whites Road.

The Arch has hung up his collar, so I am cautious about asking him to come to the University of the Free State to receive an honorary degree acknowledging his powerful contribution to making this new country, and for being the conscience of an unequal world for justice and reconciliation. As usual, he sees the bigger picture and how important this event is, not only for the UFS but also for the country.

There is a generation of wise, decent, patient and embracing men and women who are retiring from public life and passing into old age. Some of them have already left us. I think of the gracious Congress Mbata, the professor at Cornell who taught me and a founder member of the ANC Youth League, who died in exile.

There are many others, like Chabani Manganyi and the late Es'kia Mphahlele, the last of the great intellectuals who wrote about this country.

Even if they do nothing, the fact that the Arch and Nelson Mandela are still there brings comfort and reassurance in the midst of all the noise.

From a boy to his old man

Take the baton and lead

16 June 2010

A boy who grows up without a father will have problems. The man you call 'Dad' plays a powerful role in your life, even though you seldom notice it while growing up. He is like you.

You look up to him. He seems to know what he's doing and he takes care of you in ways different from those of your mother. He plays soccer, cricket or rugby with you after work. He is, of course, better at these games than you, but you suspect he sometimes allows you to bowl him out or score a goal behind his back to make you, his young son, feel good.

The more you and your father play games together, the better you get and the older he gets. Gradually, you genuinely beat him in whatever sport you play in the backyard of your home. Your old man notices that change and smiles acknowledgment of your growth and development.

You look for him at your school's prize giving or the sports match in which you play. Yes, Mom is there, but it's different for a boy when his dad is there. He comes in late, rushing from work, and when you see him, you show off because you want your dad to notice you, even though he does anyway.

As a boy you notice that other boys like to talk about their dads. 'My dad can ...' they boast in turn. 'But my dad can ...' you add to the conversation. This is what boys do; if they're not talking about girls, they're boasting about their dads. If the dads only knew what was being claimed in their name.

You notice how your dad is respected in the community. People come to him for advice. He always seems to have an answer.

Every now and again, he peers over your shoulder as you do your homework and completes an expression in your English assignment: 'Uneasy lies the head ...' Dad adds easily, '... that wears the crown.' You shyly scratch out your attempted answer, even though it rhymed and made logical sense: '... whose pillow hath fallen from the bed.'

By the time you wake up in the morning, he has already left for work to 'earn money for the family', Mom says when you ask why Dad leaves so early.

He never raises his voice to your mother. When they argue, which is rare, he backs down first.

On Thursdays, he comes home early and makes dinner. You like it when Dad makes dinner because he always makes more food and adds something special; only he makes that yellow rice with the raisins and cinnamon.

Mom makes the rules in the house, but Dad is your 'partner in crime'. He will take you for an ice cream before dinner, but you have to promise not to tell. 'Mum's the word!' he'll say, an expression whose playful double meaning you discover only years later.

Dad is your refuge when there is trouble. The boy at the corner of the street punched you on the way back from school with a jab that would have made any boxer proud. 'Wait till my dad comes home from work!' you threaten as you run for home. 'You're in big trouble, man!' you shout, clutching your bleeding nose. The Muhammad Ali wannabe is unperturbed by this threat.

Dad hardly makes it through the front door to slump in his chair when you blurt out: 'Mickey hit me!' Your chest swells with pride and expectation as you two 'men' stride, seemingly in slow motion like those dudes in the Westerns, to the corner of the street. You catch Mickey off-guard, his back towards you and your dad, as he plays marbles on the ground.

Mickey is in genuine shock but cannot run because the way is blocked from where he is sitting. Then your dad does something strange and unexpected.

He grabs Mickey and hugs him: 'I want you two to get along, Mickey. OK, my boy?' Mickey nods with relief. He never touches you again.

You stand by your old dad's bed and see his life ebb away. He has left you the wonderful gifts of love and respect. As you bury your father, you realise for the first time that you are like him, and that the baton has been passed to you to lead, as he did, with your own son.

I miss the old man. Happy Father's Day, everyone.

Leadership comes from within

Clarity of purpose matters

3 March 2010

Even to the most disinterested observer of South African society, it is abundantly clear that our country has a crisis of leadership. This is not simply a crisis of political leadership, but also a crisis of parental leadership, corporate leadership, religious leadership and educational leadership.

What I wish to do is share some life experiences about leadership in a troubled country – positive and negative lessons about leadership that make an enduring difference.

I have learnt that in leadership, clarity of purpose matters. Every day I go to work with two simple goals: to enable my students to learn to live together; and to ensure that in the heart of the country we build a university that insists on high-quality education for young graduates.

Nothing else matters. I know what I need to do, and I will move heaven and earth to accomplish these goals. To be sure, I have millions of little things to do, like balance the institutional budget. But there is a broader purpose, and being clear about that purpose is fundamental to strong leadership.

In a crisis, exemplary leadership matters. From all my years as a school teacher and as a university teacher, I know only one thing for sure, and that is that young people do not really listen to us. Rather, they observe us and imitate us. Your staff will not follow you whole-heartedly unless your life as a leader is worth following in the first place. When the chips are down, followers look to leaders not for all the answers, but for pillars of assurance and certainty of direction. Your example is crucial.

I have learnt that leadership is not only technical and muscular; it is also spiritual and emotional. The textbooks are wrong. Strong leaders are in touch with their own emotions and those of their followers. They know that the bottom line can only be achieved by relating to the spiritual and emotional lives of people.

In divided communities, equanimity of leadership matters. When you make choices as a leader based on race and favour one group over the next, then you lose the commitment and the morale of the other side. Even-handed leadership acknowledges the humanity of all followers, irrespective of what they look like, or what they believe.

Most white South Africans know that corrective action is necessary; but do it with humility and with understanding. And do not believe the lie that leadership choices in South Africa represent a racial zero-sum game. Correct in ways that include. This is an art, and the secret of wise leadership.

In difficult times, courage of conviction matters. Courageous leadership is in short supply. Leaders often do what is expedient, not what is right. And that is why, when strong winds blow, leaders topple so easily. People will sometimes criticise and dismiss you for taking a tough stand, but do the right thing and they will come to respect you, even if they disagree with you.

The most important preparation for leadership in a broken country is the acknowledgment of one's own brokenness. No leader can be perfect; that is a relief. But good leaders are aware of their weaknesses and readily admit to their own sense of struggle with history, memory and identity. In the language of the Cold War, good leaders recognise our mutual vulnerability in a dangerous and divided country.

I've learnt that leadership that overcomes division has to be countercultural leadership. I often listen to my white brothers and sisters talk about Nelson Mandela. What they admire him for most is that, as a leader, he came out of prison without bitterness.

The expectation, a reasonable one, was bitterness and vengeance. He acted against expectations by demonstrating countercultural leadership. To be a strong leader, do what people do not expect; love those you are expected to hurt; forgive those who do not deserve it. Surprise your followers by generosity when it is least expected. Make your leadership appeal not to racial solidarity, but to human solidarity.

Simply put, there can be no social change without personal change. Our salvation will not lie with governmental leadership (which is increasingly a parasitic leadership), but with the profound leadership that each of us brings to our communities, organisations and country.

This is an edited version of a speech at the City Mission Dialogue: 'Critical Conversations on Becoming a Nation', held in Cape Town in March 2010.

Ask not for whom Bill toils

An example in school leadership

2 December 2009

When Bill Schroder finally leaves his office this month, South Africa will have lost its most sincere school principal.

The man is tall in stature and in character, the complete headmaster that we teach our university students about in school leadership textbooks. His masterpiece is, without question, the country's most distinguished public high school: Pretoria Boys' High School.

'Don't let all your achievements go to your head,' I jokingly admonished a school meeting at Boys' High, 'after all, your only contribution to national culture is two hookers.'

Bill did not laugh, even as the audience fell apart, for those two boys – Mahlatse 'Chiliboy' Ralepelle and John Smit – are his two proudest sons who, in their leadership of the national rugby team, exemplify the kind of education offered by Pretoria Boys' High.

This is the only school in South Africa where I would walk across the grounds as a stranger and the boys, going in different directions, would stop dead in their tracks and greet me with 'Good morning, sir'. None of that childishness, that peering over your teenage shoulder to check whether it's cool to greet the stranger.

This was part and parcel of what it meant to be at Boys' High – you were a gentleman even if it broke your stride running to the next class. Such behaviour in teenage boys does not come by accident; it is taught through the impeccable leadership of the school master, and that is William E. Schroder.

I tested Bill Schroder once, eager to know if he could step out of the frame of a middle-class boys' school within walking distance of South Africa's premier research university.

A friend discovered a young talent in a school in an informal settlement and it was clear to me that if this boy could go to a quality high school, such as Boys' High, he could rise to fulfil his talent and do something great with his life.

So I called Bill, knowing full well that his selection of Grade 7s was done months in advance and that he had to turn away hundreds of children. Without blinking, and without money readily at hand, Bill allowed access to this child wonder from Orange Farm; it is a gesture I will never forget.

Bill Schroder does transformation quietly. For years, he has run one of the most racially integrated schools in South Africa. He offers leadership opportunities to black and white, middle class and poor; the kind of school culture that allows boys like Chiliboy and John equal opportunities, and to excel academically and in sport.

Among the groups that flourish at this historically English-speaking school are Afrikaans-speakers, and one of the most astounding high school speeches I ever heard was in Afrikaans by a mother-tongue speaker. In Bill's school, there is no prejudice, only embrace.

I have to be honest and say that I was often envious about the ease with which black and white boys at this school became lifelong friends because of the environment Bill created there.

His period of history straddled the transition to democracy and he made sure that disadvantaged children not only entered the school, but also excelled in accelerated learning programmes.

Like every other top school in the country, Pretoria Boys' High delivered the academic results. But what made this school special was the value added, that extra dimension to learning and living that makes good schools great.

Year after year, I saw clumsy boys transformed into courageous young men, uncertain youths changed into confident leaders, and boys from economically unequal backgrounds level the playing field through equal learning opportunities.

After twenty years of service to Pretoria Boys' High School, Bill Schroder leaves a legacy of thousands of boys who have passed through his hands into leadership in every field in this country.

Well done, Bill. I can now confer on you that deeply meaningful Afrikaans title for teachers of stature: *Meester*.

The sound of your own voice

Can you hear your anger?

11 November 2009

Once you've met Magteld, you'll never forget her.

It's not because she is deaf. It's because of her unbelievable enthusiasm for life, her commitment to her studies (two master's degrees in hand) and her determination to be heard.

So I felt really chuffed that she had invited me to the Big Day – that special moment when she would hear clearly for the first time.

The room is quiet. The small audience waits in rapt expectation. Where is the man with the fancy equipment? The cochlear implant has been in her ear for about a month; that, say the experts, is the minimum time before the device can be activated.

The media are here in force (the hype has been building up around this day for some time). So is Miss Deaf SA, Vicki Fourie, herself struggling with hearing loss.

My learned colleagues sit behind a glass window and, like me, they must have wondered: 'What if the thing doesn't work?'

Then the man with the fancy computer and the wires arrives. Representations of sound waves run across vertical bars on the computer screen. Slowly he adjusts the volume of each bar.

'Can you hear it?' he asks Magteld.

'More, please more,' she pleads as the vibrations hit the ear. Eventually, all the bars have been set.

Now the big moment arrives. The computer man has to activate the combined sound. At this point Magteld asks him to stand back: 'My professor will do this,' she says.

I obey the instruction and move towards a chair alongside my colleague. I hold her hand and with the other press the 'Activate' bar on the screen.

Nothing happens. Then, suddenly, Magteld rocks backward in her chair as the strength of unfamiliar sound hits her eardrum.

'*Ek hoor my eie stem!*' she shouts. 'I can hear my own voice.'

Tears in the room. Joy on the face of my hearing colleague. A simple sensation taken for granted. A life changed instantly. Here, in the medical school of the University of the Free State, yet another miracle happens in the life of an ordinary citizen.

In the past few weeks, I have thought a lot about that simple but profound statement: 'I can hear my own voice.'

I am convinced that we seldom take the time to hear what we sound like.

We are an angry people. Whether it is the noise around the leadership of Eskom, or the treatment of Ms Caster Semenya, or the fate of a politician, we scream and shout with anger.

We have become deaf to our own voices.

For the first time, I understand how the widespread xenophobic attacks last year could have happened as we carry our anger on our sleeves. This anger, unleashed, can turn otherwise peaceful citizens into murderous villains in seconds.

We should be very worried about this. No wonder we are among the most murderous nations in the world. Small wonder then that women are exposed to danger in so many homes because of angry men. Should we be surprised that small children are constantly exposed to abuse, even rape, by grown men?

We are an angry people.

I expect denial. After all, we can justify our anger – our own pain matters; nobody else has pain. I am right; the other side is wrong. There is no complexity, no grey area, no subtlety – just the harsh, unforgiving and relentless noise of accusation and dismissal.

Here's the problem: anger, like most emotions, can be reproduced. The son who observes the anger of a father often becomes angry himself, assuming the same posture of abuse against women, for example.

Anger then becomes normative; it's not only how we are, it also defines who we are.

Magteld taught me something precious the other day – not only that I should not take the gift of physical hearing for granted, but also that I needed to be conscious of the danger of being deaf to my own voice.

At the crossroads once more

The complexities of reconciliation

28 October 2009

The young woman who sat behind me to the left hardly made an impression. I remember her as petite, quiet most of the time, and very interested in the class on African studies.

Like so many of the young American men and women in this class, they were learning about Africa so that they could volunteer to work in countries such as Liberia and Tanzania and, of course, the hot topic of that period, South Africa.

Even though I was a postgraduate student in that class, and therefore older, I was enjoying the time studying with these young people, who were inspired to serve in NGOs, the Peace Corps and various church communities.

The next time I heard about the young woman who had sat behind me was that she had been killed on the streets of a Cape Town township by a group of angry black men who crushed her skull. Her name was Amy Biehl.

What really struck me about that event was not only the horrible death of an idealistic young woman, but the spirit of her parents, who had just lost a treasured daughter.

They could have proclaimed her innocence for, after all, she was working in upliftment programmes for disadvantaged communities.

They could have made much of the fact that she was American and not a white South African, and could not therefore be blamed for the execution of apartheid, let alone have been a beneficiary of that evil system.

But the Biehls stood tall, determined not to be bitter, but to offer a better way for resolving hurt and loss.

During the past week I have thought often about those moments in our history when ordinary people were able to rise above retribution and seek reconciliation. When great men dived into the midst of an angry crowd to save a man or woman from death by burning. When a man, put away for 27 years, could come out of prison willing to embrace. When mothers who lost their sons could stretch out the hand of acceptance to the police chief on whose watch these terrible things happened.

But reconciliation is complex.

There are no predetermined rules. Legal prescription cannot mend hearts. Political injunction cannot force change. There is no cookbook recipe in the daily and difficult pursuit of being human.

Sometimes the perpetrator is beaten up by his victims on making the approach. Sometimes the approach made by the victims in search of peace receives no response. Often, the perpetrator stands fast in denial, doing irreparable harm to others and him or herself. When, in rare circumstances, perpetrator and victim meet together to acknowledge the pain inflicted and received, something magical happens.

What we do know, is that failure to reconcile at crucial moments in history can destroy a nation. We can build such deep divides in anger that it might take generations to overcome. The consequence is the Middle East, Rwanda or Northern Ireland.

The biggest stumbling block is self-righteousness – that sense that we all are non-racial angels who never lash out in anger at, or harbour bitterness towards, or harm others.

A friend said something interesting the other day: the one pervasive myth is that no whites supported apartheid; the other is that all blacks were against apartheid. The truth is we are all tainted by our terrible past. Many of us would like to see full and permanent retribution, not reconciliation.

Most South Africans would rather hang murderers than let them live.

The expression that we are 'all for reconciliation', while spouting anger and bitterness, is therefore unhelpful.

We again stand at such a moment in our history. How we move forward will determine not only the resolution of our problems at present, but also the kind of society we will have in the future.

Noise will not help.

Learn to escape the parent trap

Inspire your children to embrace learning

10 September 2009

Setting a good example trumps having to maintain discipline.

My dad was a hawker. In fact, he was many things. He once laboured as a domestic worker. For many years he drove a van, collecting and delivering laundry for Nannucci Dry Cleaners in Cape Town. Towards the end of his career he was a messenger for a Cape Town shipping company. His life ended as a full-time missionary serving poverty-stricken people in the Karoo.

But what I remember about this man called Abraham (whose wife was Sarah, really, who bore a son called Isaac, really) was the enormous impact he had on my life choices as a child growing up on the dangerous Cape Flats.

Some time ago, one of my doctoral students conducted an impressive study on ten of the most successful black scientists in South Africa. She wanted to know why these remarkable scholars obtained PhDs despite the social and educational disadvantage they had endured during the years of apartheid.

More bluntly, why did these scientists achieve the highest qualifications in their fields when so many of their peers did not?

What my student found was that there were many factors that accounted for the success of the ten scientists, but it was hard to nail down the factors common to all of them. One thing did stand out, however, and that was a powerful parental figure in the home.

- This parent did not necessarily have much education, but valued education highly.
- The parent worked night and day to ensure that the meagre resources were available to enable the child to succeed.
- The parent insisted on routines, such as homework and school attendance, no matter what.
- Whenever the child would so much as think about skipping school or escaping homework, there stood the parent, larger than life, to prevent the child from straying into waywardness.

For all ten scientists, it was parental authority that had made the difference.

So often I have seen the converse to be true in my work with young people. Show me a troubled boy or a traumatised girl, and nine times out of ten I will be able to show you an absentee father or a negligent mother. In an era in which so many of our schools do not present teachers as powerful, influential role models – who often compensate for parents' inadequacies, or complement their role – mothers and fathers become even more crucial in determining the fate of their children.

Which brings me back to Abie, as they called my father, and his educational influence on our lives as

179

children. Perhaps it was the pride with which he referred to his 'JC' (junior certificate – then a serious qualification) from Livingstone High School that impressed me. Maybe it was his undisguised joy when his children did well at school.

I suspect it was also his unusual way of telling you 'there is room for improvement', even when you scored full marks in a test. It could have been the memory games he would play with us as children. He demonstrated the enormous capacity of his memory by reciting Bible verses or recalling the registration numbers of all his friends' cars.

I remember how, when I was in primary school, he would be sipping tea and, without warning, throw a line at me: 'A stitch in time ...' I would jump to attention: '... saves nine.' But my trouble would start when he shot back: 'And what does that mean?'

Whatever it was, he had the knack of making sure that, as a child, you understood the value and joy of education.

Most parents get this part wrong. They lecture children endlessly on doing their homework. They throw major tantrums when the results on the report cards are not what they expected from their children. They threaten kids with everything from no more weekends with friends to pulling out the TV cables.

Discipline is good, but when children equate education with threats, and schooling with punishment, don't expect them to enjoy learning and aspire to further education.

It is the simple things parents do between tests and examinations, like the marvel they express when observing a loaded plane lift off the runway, the questions they pose about a scientific discovery, the joy they demonstrate when recalling a favourite poem, and the delight they exude when solving a puzzle.

For parents to inspire children to learn, they need not be highly schooled themselves. All they need is to enjoy learning themselves.

TALK ABOUT SOCIETY

*'Does South Africa really belong
to all who live in it?'*

Little Spirit

Strength against all odds

Not yet published in English

I have never been on anyone's bucket list before, though perhaps secretly on more than one person's hit list. So the announcement by my secretary that a high school teenager was flying from Cape Town to see me this past Monday brought a groan. This was the first day of the holidays and I had two books to work on and several other smaller pieces of writing whose deadlines were coming up fast. 'You have to see her,' my unusually pushy secretary said firmly, 'you're on her bucket list.'

Fortunately I had seen the movie by that name, and only a creep would deny a dying child a meeting request. 'Who is she?' I inquired.

And then it all fell into place. This youngster with the appropriate Afrikaans name, *Geesie* ('Little Spirit'), crossed my path during a marketing drive to schools in the Western Cape earlier this year. The principal of D.F. Malan High School had introduced me to this young woman who suffered from devastating cancer of the brain that had rendered her blind. During that visit, I had embraced the young soul and started an impromptu message of encouragement and support, when she interrupted me. Little Spirit then gave me a message of hope that I remember to this day. Of course, I would interrupt my writing vacation for Geesie Theron.

So off to Mugg & Bean where Geesie, her mother and her much larger twin sister were already waiting. Here's the problem. Apart from the fact that she is small, thin and blind, there is nothing about Geesie that suggests that she might not live much longer. Geesie has plans for Christmas; she excels in her academic work; she is working on two drawing books, and she meets famous people like Ryk Neethling and Jacques Kallis. There is a spring in her step as she walks, gently guided by her mother through the mall crowds, towards the rented car.

For more than an hour around a plate of potato wedges and strong coffee, we laugh at the world. Geesie leads the discussions on everything from boyfriends, to sports, to university studies, to English-Afrikaans translations, to nonsense. There is no morbid talk here about death and dying; for Geesie, the world is not enough. I leave this meeting, my spirits lifted.

This has been a difficult year for our beloved country, South Africa. It ends the way it started. Racist venom from prominent figures like Steve Hofmeyr and Annelie Botes, both defended with some energy in parts of the Afrikaans press. Terrible murders, often wiping out families from Lindley in the eastern Free State to Mpola, near Mari-annhill in kwaZulu-Natal. Night after night the evening news informs or reminds us of another baby or teenager raped, sometimes in bushes, at other times on school playgrounds. Political parties cannot meet without chairs being thrown around or fistfights breaking out; delegations are in conflict, and there are fights for positions among comrades in the courts. Not a day passes without another report about snouts in the tender troughs.

Two more public universities are subjected to government investigations. In the one, unbelievably, not only do external members of the council get paid to attend meetings, but the internal members (that is, the staff members) also receive cash for showing up! What happens in such cases, of course, is that you try to arrange as many meetings as possible; the more meetings, the more money you get paid.

The report of the assessor is readily available on the Internet and shows that substantial amounts of time in meetings of the council – the highest authority in a university – were spent not on matters of research and scholarship, or on teaching and intellectual life, but on the compensation of members of this august body.

In another university, irregularities in tenders again come under the spotlight of an upcoming investigation. So here's the truth: even universities, those supposed places of higher learning, are now happy hunting grounds for what Mr Vavi of Cosatu correctly calls a 'predatory elite'.

But Geesie reminded me that there is another South Africa, one seldom found in the sludgy newspapers or on the evening news. It is a South Africa in which the majority of its people are decent, hardworking, respectful and hopeful, despite their circumstances. Most people in this country are neither racists nor crooks. Most will, no matter the hardships of personal lives or domestic economies, enjoy the ordinary and priceless benefits of being alive, of gathering with family members, of sharing a simple meal on Christmas Day. To the millions of Little Spirits out there, happy holidays!

Tribal lines still firmly drawn

We slide into different camps when confronted with crises

17 November 2010

'I am a detribalised South African,' said a good friend without a hint of the enormous significance of these words.

His casual statement caught me off-guard, for this kind of acknowledgment is rare in South Africa. It is a high state of existence when you no longer behave towards, or react to, or think of yourself or others in tribal terms, but on the basis of a principle, commitment or value that transcends primordial ties.

During the struggle days when we were treated to heroic accounts of the exiled ANC, a starting point in our education was 1912. Then and now, I find that episode in history compelling – the ANC was founded with the express purpose of breaking down tribal differences, and of uniting its followers around common struggles for rights and representation.

No doubt, the ANC faithful will soon return to the sacred founding site, Bloemfontein, to commemorate the Party's visionary beginnings as the South African Native National Congress.

I have been dealing with some angry people lately, and what always strikes me is the ease with which we slide into tribal camps whenever we are confronted with a crisis.

Logic gives way to emotion; argument to anger. The evidence does not matter; after all, what can you expect from Indians, they steal; or from whites, they're racist; or from Africans, they're incompetent.

As distasteful as these descriptions may be, so many South Africans keep these essentialist notions of other people firmly in their heads, even if they are not articulated as such in respectable company. Tribal lines are firmly drawn, and hardly crossed.

The day I will believe South Africans are transformed is the day a white man stands up among his peers, in public, and condemns an offensive act towards black people because it is wrong.

In all my life, I have not seen this once. Why? Because tribal loyalty is so firmly in place. You do not go against your own, and if you did, you would be labelled something really nasty and excluded from all further social gatherings of the tribe. The judgment would be swift and harsh.

There is a price to pay for standing on loyalty to truth, rather than to tribe.

Notice what happens when a letter from a Muslim reader appears in any South African newspaper condemning Jews in the state of Israel for their treatment of the Palestinians. With clockwork predictability, the next day there will be two or three letters by Jewish readers condemning the Muslim reader for being irrational, or worse. It works the other way as well.

I find this very boring. No thought, only emotion; no attempt to understand, only condemnation. The world is divided neatly among the protagonists, as between the tribes of Good and the tribes of Evil.

Transformation will have come to South Africa when a black man supports a white man in public on a matter of principle, rather than to side with the black offender simply because the brother is black.

God knows, we are a long, long way from this kind of maturity.

The black person who acts independently, who thinks for himself, must be called a nasty name for refusing to bow to the imperative of tribal loyalty. Of course, you're not really black, for there is something in your skin that would have had you naturally taking a position on the darker side, if you know what I mean.

One of the most common responses I get to taking public positions that fall outside of tribal affiliation is the request for a private meeting, at which point a black or white person will say: 'I agree with you on X, but it is difficult for me to say so in public.'

I have two feelings about this. One, respect for the person for at least having a position on principle. Two, sadness, for the lack of courage to speak or stand up in public is what constrains the pursuit of what we far too glibly call a 'non-racial democracy'.

No need to fall into conceptual perplexity with these words, as my colleagues at the English universities are wont to do: non-racialism simply means the building of a society in which our referential framework for thought, decisions and self-referencing is not tribe.

We might never get there if the state keeps insisting that we tick our 'tribe' on official forms of all kinds.

My friend who makes the claim that he is detribalised has reached the state of non-racial nirvana. I hope I too can get there one day.

No playing the race card right

Calling a person racist is akin to shouting 'fire' in a cinema

10 November 2010

This week, a young man whom I know narrowly escaped death after an attempted suicide. On the day he tried to end his pain, he was found innocent after a malicious attempt to label him as a 'racist' for something he did not do.

The media had converged on the young white man, identifying and condemning him for an attack on a black person that turned out to be false. But for months after the savage media attack on the youngster, he had to bear the burden of public ridicule, suspicion from his friends, and what will no doubt be permanent damage to his reputation. His mind, body and spirit were crushed by the public accusation, and he could take it no more.

I tell this story because of the alarming ease with which we accuse and destroy good people with the very serious charge of racism. People who do this know how such a charge can emotionally destroy a human being. It is the foulest of charges, especially in the wake of our terrible past. You cannot 'prove' that you're not a racist because you will always sound guilty in the mind of the accuser and the many South Africans who are ready to judge you as guilty on the flimsiest piece of evidence of racial discrimination. It is like witch hunting in the northern

193

provinces – accuse the person of being a witch, then destroy her, and maybe get to the facts after the funeral.

Do not for one moment believe that the accused are always white. I was shocked to observe on television how a senior member of the ruling party accused a distinguished black woman, one who had made many sacrifices for our country, as being against 'transformation'. That is the new code word for racists: they are anti-transformation.

In this careless use of language, any disagreement with another person on a matter of principle or strategy draws out the charge of anti-transformation, or racism.

Corrupt people play this race card. Incompetent people hide behind the race card. Tribalists love the race card. These kinds of people appoint themselves as the high priests of racial equality; they alone care about fairness, non-discrimination and equity.

And, as I see almost daily, when as a black man you confront these reckless people about playing the race card, they have an even better card in their pockets: the ethnic card. 'You do not really understand the problems of Africans,' risked a friend who possesses much less melanin than I do.

We swallow the apartheid narrative of racial essences, neatly packaged into four categories of human existence (white, coloured, African and Indian), with alarming facility. This singular narrative of 'whites as racists' is going to cost us dearly into the future, and some might argue that it is already causing great harm in the present.

Take the front pages of the last one hundred issues of the major Afrikaans daily published out of Johannesburg, and you will see the daily reporting on white murder, trauma and grief. Alarmist? Yes. But slowly in the minds of ordinary white citizens there builds the kind of racial resentment I witness daily.

The problem of racism is real. Anyone who thought that centuries of racial domination would dissipate with the advent of majority rule is seriously misguided. Not only should individual acts of racism concern us; so too should its institutionalisation in the practices of social entities, such as churches, schools and sporting bodies.

And yet no one can refute that South Africa has made enormous strides in becoming a more normal society in terms of race relations. Only if you lived through the worst days of apartheid can you appreciate the progress made.

What threatens that progress is the mindless racial provocation, calling someone racist as if this is some playful excess that has no consequences for human lives.

So what do we do about this?

Charging racism without evidence or foundation must become a crime with serious consequences; a court-enforced apology is not enough. It is, in our historical context, the equivalent of shouting 'fire' in a packed cinema when there is none.

There have to be consequences for such irresponsible acts, or the bad behaviour will continue. Nobody has the right to debase another human being through an act of racism; the same applies to those who falsely accuse another human with this dreaded charge.

Mixed messages

Does South Africa belong to all who live in it?

6 October 2010

Does South Africa really belong to all who live in it? When I first developed a sense for politics, as a teenager on the Cape Flats and wallowing in anger, this was the one clause in the Freedom Charter that upset me: 'South Africa belongs to all who live in it, black and white.'

They (whites) came from elsewhere; they caused all our problems; they took the land and exterminated indigenous people, such as the San; they uprooted, disenfranchised, tortured and killed black people at will. So, how on earth could the Congress Alliance even think of such a concession?

In the course of time, and as I became aware of the broad front of resistance and solidarity across the colour line, this clause for me became the single most admired assertion in the charter.

When I learnt of John Harris's execution (a story, by the way, told very movingly in David Beresford's recent book, *Truth is a Strange Fruit*), of Beyers Naudé's sacrifice, of Ruth First's martyrdom, anger gave way to admiration.

A response to the inaugural lecture of the Ahmed Kathrada Foundation, delivered by Deputy President Kgalema Motlanthe at Wits University, Johannesburg, on 1 October 2010.

That memorable photograph of those four women of different shades walking confidently up the steps of the Union Building in 1956 to protest against the deviance of apartheid remains, in my judgment, the most moving image of non-racial solidarity this country has ever produced.

But something has gone wrong, especially since 1999. And, depending on where you spend your time working and living, you might be more or less conscious of the racial fault lines opening up across the land.

During the past year, I have spent much of my time in rural and agricultural South Africa, far away from the cosmopolitanism of Johannesburg or Durban. I spend time at formerly white universities, to which students from rural South Africa often come, and at which racial divisions between white and black are more deeply ingrained than elsewhere.

I listen carefully to the voices of white and black parents, students and communities up and down South Africa, and I am troubled. Events such as Reitz, Ventersdorp, Waterkloof or Skierlik are **not** examples of spontaneous combustion.

Dismissing these horrific events as 'racism' does not advance understanding, let alone solutions. Rather, they represent underlying lava currents of racial discontent that constantly threaten our young democracy, and which will, from time to time, burst through the social surface like an erupting volcano doing huge damage to our quest for a non-racial society.

Why is this happening? I believe we lost ground with the project of nation building in the post-Mandela period. Our language started to change; our sense of others started to shift. Angry and undisciplined voices emerged all over the land, and the politics of accusation and insult replaced earlier efforts at dialogue.

We adopted angry public positions that conveyed, especially to young white South Africans, a sense of our anger.

In the name of equity and redistribution, we sent messages throughout society that were interpreted as politically exclusionary, rather than as calling for a commonality of purpose in rebuilding on the ruins of our shattered past. That we achieved little of either equity or redistribution is a separate, though critically important, issue.

What we have failed to do is build a strong and sustainable understanding across the nation, as we did briefly for the Soccer World Cup, that 'together' means black and white – all of us – are together in developing this economy, this democracy and this society.

Of course, we have a Constitution that guarantees certain rights and policies that, on paper, are not discriminatory. But here we need to be very careful.

We must distinguish official directives (the formal claims of a policy) from the emotional understanding of a policy by ordinary citizens. Few people have major gripes with our national policies or laws; in fact, you might have noticed that the people who most often cite the Constitution in their claims are those on the right of the political spectrum. What divides us are not our policies, but the secondary messages sent out about them.

What do I mean by this tricky term 'secondary messages'? I mean the subtle, and sometimes not-too-subtle, cues, suggestions, actions and symbols communicated not through official statements, but through dispersed segments of society that often speak for or, at the very least, are not repudiated by, the powerful.

Messages such as: 'The struggle was/is about black people in general and Africans in particular'; 'Only blacks need apply' and 'Despite your academic results, we reserve places at medical school on a sliding scale from white to Indian to coloured to African'.

Messages such as: 'Only an African can become president of the country'; 'It is a matter of time before your farms will be taken from you and given to the dispossessed' and 'We will punish you if you do not get your employment equity commitments right soon'.

These secondary messages are often much more powerful than the primary or official messages that emanate from the political centre of the country.

I could cite many other examples, but here is the good news. South Africans are emotional people, an insight recognised by Nelson Mandela and President Jacob Zuma.

Strong leaders, who lead in the aftermath of the world's longest surviving racial order, know that we do not have to make a choice between equity and equality, or between redistribution and reconciliation.

We can, and must, do both. We must recapture that sense of grace and generosity, not in our policies but in our practice.

This is not an easy or popular way to go – for grace, a friend reminds me, is always scandalous, and generosity risks rejection. But this is what bold and courageous leadership is about; we can afford nothing less.

Our leaders must be careful not to think that, by attending to the extremes of society – such as the whites of Orania, or Eugene de Kock in Pretoria Central Prison – we can build respect, tolerance and collaboration in 'middle South Africa', the country of those ordinary citizens among whom the quest for hope and healing remains, and where the desire to make a difference can still be harnessed by the government and civil society.

Our starting point should be different, however. Perhaps the primary message should be that the struggle for development is about South Africans in general, and human beings in particular.

Our broken promises

As we celebrate our miracles, let us not forget those we've left behind

22 September 2010

The 93-year-old woman walked towards the elevated graduation stage last week with a firm step. She let go of her attendant, determined to walk across the stage alone. Head held high, she strode ahead to receive her doctorate in theology. It is not true that her thesis was on the resurrection.

As she descended the stairs, the large crowd at the University of the Free State leapt to its feet like one. Thunderous applause. Something special had just happened. Here was a living testimony to a dying policy: lifelong learning.

Next across the stage was a blind undergraduate student. He needed assistance on the narrow plank that runs between the announcement of your name, the chancellor's cap on your head and the ribbon sash draped around your neck. Once again, thunderous applause. The audience knows that for this blind student to have achieved his degree, he had to work twice as hard as other students.

He had to fight for his lecture notes in Braille. He had to risk walking across a campus designed for the sighted student. He had to agitate for classrooms and elevators fitted for students with disabilities. Today he walks proudly.

I have done this academic duty called graduation a few hundred times before, but today I feel teary. Here in central South Africa, away from the din of succession politics and the greed of the powerful, small miracles are happening that seldom make it into the headlines.

I lose track of the number of postgraduate students from other African countries receiving their degrees from the University of the Free State this week. I cannot help but notice the rich integration of audience and graduates in an institution the media relentlessly portrays through the lens of race. The students crossing the stage come from every continent, and the rapture of graduation day spills over onto the lawns of the university where we drink tea with spouses, parents, children and relatives who have travelled in convoy to witness the great day.

Despite the joy of graduation I am also deeply saddened, for I know that there are millions of bright young people who will never witness this glorious day.

This is the same week in which Sadtu Gauteng threatens to return to strike action, now only days way from the final examination of our Grade 12 learners. You can rest assured that not a single striker in this motley crowd has their child in a targeted school. They must surely know that their strike plans have already doomed another generation of young black children to a life of unemployment; they surely know that many of the poorest Grade 12 learners now stand no chance of qualifying for university entrance. How can anyone be this callous?

A good friend who is a leader in the automotive industry tells a disturbing story about his recent visit to Japan. He told his seniors in Tokyo about their plans to scale up the production of motor cars in the wake of the strike in the manufacturing sector; by the end of December, production would be back on track. His Japanese bosses took little interest in his plans; they had a much more serious concern: 'How on earth can you close your schools?'

To the Japanese, and indeed any productive economy outside Africa, this is an abiding puzzle. How can you sacrifice the future of your youth and the future of your democracy on the altar of immediacy ('We want it all, and we want it now')?

Nations with vision think about the distant future, the building blocks that must be put in place now for economy and democracy. Wise leaders look beyond electoral cycles; they worry about future generations. The education of a child can never be traded for the salary of a worker; it is as simple and noble as that.

What the Japanese apparently also could not understand, is how we could shut down hospitals during the recent strike. Their perspective is historical: 'Even during mortal wars, there is an agreement on the part of the warring factions that the hospitals would not be targeted in attack.' Maybe this explains our problem as South Africans. We did not have mortal wars on national soil during the past century.

So, the next time you go to a graduation ceremony, think not only of the determination to succeed of the aged and the blind, and of the enormous sacrifices of parents and spouses to be able to witness this high point in the lives of their loved ones. Think also of the wastage, the loss of talent, the millions who could have been there but stood no chance because of the callousness of our society.

The violence within us

The pain of past lies

25 August 2010

'They lied to us, they lied to us, they lied to us!' The bearded white man shook with emotion as he repeated these words after the talk I had just delivered at a Men's Convention in the poor white community of Elsburg in the south of Johannesburg.

This was the second men's convention that I was privileged to address on successive weekends. One thing is crystal clear: there is a deep and unremitting pain among middle-aged men about the past, about their participation in it, and especially about that unspoken war in which white men were conscripted into military service to do things that few dare speak about.

Do not be deceived by the poorly written books by former soldiers with bravado and self-justification lacing the pages; it is an attempt to retain sanity as these men come to terms with official lies.

What are the lies the bearded man is talking about? It was the lie that they were fighting terrorists when they were fighting their brothers and sisters. It was the lie that their country had a democracy to be defended when what we had was a pigmentocracy that was indefensible. It was the lie that you could repress the democratic instincts of people deprived of land, life and the right to vote, and get away with it. It was the lie, of course, that white rule was about defending Christian civilisation against godless communism.

Over these two weekends, seven men at these two men's conventions came separately to talk with strong emotion about what they did in the past. Here was a trauma that remains concealed from public and even familial view, and that could burst into open rage and inflict great pain on the individual and society if not dealt with.

Which brings me to the 'public servant' strikes (the term itself sounds laughable, given the destruction under way) in the beloved country. What should scare South Africans is not the strike itself; after all, our democracy allows for citizens to participate in peaceful protests.

What should concern us is how protest cultures that are vicious and violent are the norm. In other words, the foundations of our culture and society are permanently changing, so that it is no longer enough to have differences with other people; we must go further and destroy, break down, threaten and attack the people and institutions with which we disagree.

There is another view on all of this. Africa's most distinguished social scientist, Mahmood Mamdani from Makerere University in Uganda, likes to make this important point: 'The present is not its own explanation.' In other words, when you witness the violent behaviour of strikers, the reasons for such actions lie in the distant past, not in the observable behaviour of the moment.

The question that must be asked, therefore, is this: how did we come to be such violent people? Of course, our country was born out of conquest and violence centuries back. The apartheid government tortured and killed people, making violence part of our societal culture. Put differently, violence became institutionalised in our society.

That is why outsiders to the rainbow nation cannot understand why a democratic government would use the methodologies of the previous government – rubber bullets and tear gas – on the people who voted it into power.

When we placed tyres around the necks of people suspected of being informers for the previous government, we contributed to the conditions for institutionalised violence that remain with us today.

Rather than simply condemn violence – and we should – we must ask the question: 'Where does it come from?' The present is not its own explanation.

But we are not victims of our past, whether as one-time conscripts in apartheid's army or as present-day strikers in our post-apartheid democracy. We can change this behaviour, difficult as it may be. Talks about complex social questions must always be preferred to demonstration. Peaceful protests must become the norm, not violent protest cultures. The lines for decent behaviour must be firmly drawn.

We fool ourselves, however, if we think that simply by repressing the strikers or dismissing the trauma of former policemen and soldiers we can resolve the underlying reasons for our private and public behaviour. The violence of the present is not spontaneous combustion; it comes from somewhere.

Our commentators and officials now need to go beyond the expression of disbelief and the condemnation of terror. It is time for a national dialogue on how we came to be this way. Or expect worse.

I am a foreigner – to hatred

The dawning of human recognition

14 July 2010

In horror, I read that scores of Zimbabwean refugees were camping along the N1 highway to flee the rainbow nation, in response to threats of what would happen to them once the Soccer World Cup ended. I then found myself drawing on that profound source of intellectual inspiration, the animated film *Finding Nemo*.

Marlin, Nemo's father, drifts off by himself, despondent that he cannot find his son. Dory (the fish with Alzheimer's, as one youngster put it) begs him over and over again not to leave. Then Dory makes a telling observation about their relationship that I will never forget – his final plea to Marlin comes with the words: 'I look at you, and I'm home.'

How I wish a South African resident could look a Malawian refugee in the face and the two say to each other, 'I look at you, and I'm home.'

Dory's words speak of home not as a literal place or a strip of land, but as a heart relationship between human beings.

Anyone who has lost a mother will know what I mean; going home just isn't the same after your mother has died. Because home was not the house; it was that bond of love between mother and child.

A brilliant movie maker, Molly Blank, renders a powerful account about xenophobia in her new documentary, *Where Do I Stand?* She tells the story of the attacks on foreigners in 2008, in which sixty-two people died. The story is told through the voices of five South African youngsters, some of whom were involved in the looting and attacks.

As they reflect on their criminal deeds, the young people come to understand that those they harmed were human beings, with the same fears, anxieties and aspirations that they have.

Then something profound happens: the attackers begin to repair the damage. They make public statements of regret, but then they also take their business back to the Somalian shopkeepers, walking past the shops of native vendors to make the point. Other young people in the documentary find ways of caring for their brothers and sisters in different ways. One student hides a *makwerekwere* (a derogatory word for foreigners) in his sparse home.

The young people take a stand. Slowly but surely, black and white begin to share their homes and lives with those living between two desperate worlds: their home countries and this refugee nation.

What happens, clearly, is that the moment of human recognition dawns on these young South Africans: 'I see you, and I'm home.'

We as South Africans need to look in the mirror after this Soccer World Cup and ask ourselves an uncomfortable question: why do we celebrate Ghanaians and other

Africans on the soccer pitch but persecute them in the townships?

I saw rich and poor natives of our land weep when Luis 'Hand of God' Suárez robbed Ghana of a sure goal en route to the World Cup semi-finals. I see no such solidarity of emotion as the bloody hands of natives shove threatening letters under the shack doors of our neighbours from the region. What kind of hypocrisy is this?

This was always my fear about the wave of nationalistic fever that spread across the land during the World Cup; there is a dark side (if you will forgive the pun) to such passionate love of country – it excludes.

Our pan-African solidarity is superficial; a cosmopolitan view of the world is lacking. And for this we pay the price in blood.

Make no mistake, the people who are now pursuing foreigners could sooner or later turn on the rest of us. There will always have to be a scapegoat for misery, real or imagined. People who kill foreigners can one day quickly divide the rest of us into a 'non-' group (you complete the 'non-').

I have had my fair share of people – some very well educated – calling me 'non-' because they believe they are whiter or blacker than the rest of us. Watch out for these killers.

I am about to buy and distribute T-shirts that carry the words 'I am a foreigner'.

I am a foreigner to xenophobia, to race hatred, to stereotyping, to the physical and emotional abuse of our neighbours, to mindless patriotism. I hope millions of South Africans will wear such T-shirts.

The foreigners are us, and we are them. Find a foreigner, grab him by the shoulders and then say boldly: 'I look at you, and I'm home.'

Molly Blank's DVD on healing and hope in the wake of xenophobia, with teacher resources, can be obtained by visiting www.wheredoIstandfilm.com.

We're opening up our history

How will you answer questions about the past?

7 July 2010

The little boy of five or six years old ran just ahead of his mother from one exhibit to the next in the National War Museum in Bloemfontein. Each time he stopped at a photograph depicting the Anglo-Boer conflict, the boy would ask, '*Mamma, wat het hier gebeur?*' (Mommy, what happened here?). I was fascinated by the question, and even more intrigued by the possible answers.

So when the boy stopped right next to me, with his mother half-running to keep up with her son, he posed the stinger again: '*Wat het hier gebeur?*' The massive drawing in question showed Boer and Brit in heavy fighting, with bodies of the slain lying all over a hill in the rural Free State.

The mother, perhaps conscious of the peaked ears of the small group of visitors next to her, whispered the obvious: 'Here they were fighting again.'

The National War Museum captures one of the unspoken complexities of the new South Africa, and it is this: can a place of memory, originally constructed for purposes of Afrikaner nationalism, be transformed to reflect the ideals of a united, peaceful and democratic South Africa?

This museum, surrounded by other potent symbols of Afrikaner struggles – like the gravesite of M.T. Steyn and the *Vrouemonument* (Women's Memorial) – tries to keep up with the times.

Suddenly, there are stories inserted of black heroes of that time, like Sol Plaatje, who has his own section in the museum. At the entrance, visitors receive introductions to the museum in three languages: English, Afrikaans and Sesotho. Blacks are now very visible on each side of the struggle between Boer and Brit, though mainly as servants and soldiers.

This is definitely not what I learnt at school about what is now called the South African War, but then was named the Anglo-Boer War. This was a holy site for Afrikaner nationalists, a place where the Boer dead were counted and named for the different concentration camps, and where women and children who died at the hands of the English are memorialised in the tall spire that is the *Vrouemonument*.

One of the difficulties of telling an inclusive human story about a once-exclusive racial memory is that you can easily slip into an amoral position on matters that require intense, honest and critical engagement with the past.

So, for example, there is a separate Children's Memorial on the site. The photographs show children's suffering during the Anglo-Boer War; in the wake of the atomic bombing at Hiroshima; and there is the familiar photo of the two youths running with the body of Hector Pieterson. Good.

But there is no commentary at all on the moral and political meanings of these photographic exhibits, and not only activists of the time would balk at the description of the Soweto event as chaotic 'riots', rather than the more accepted 'uprising'. What you are witnessing, according to these memorials, is simply what happens when children are caught in the crossfire of wars.

Which brings me back to the little boy and his troubling question, which I cannot get out of my head. Would his mother have told the young boy about two white settler communities struggling over land to the exclusion of the native majority?

Would he have heard about the good Englishwoman, Emily Hobhouse, who stood up against her tribe to support and empower the still embryonic Afrikaner communities struggling to assert themselves against the British Crown?

Would the boy have heard about the hopes and dreams of black people drawn into that war, only to discover, over and over again, that they would remain in subservience and bondage for almost a century afterwards? And, most importantly, would the boy have heard the story of this tumultuous past in ways that opened his young heart to a solidarity that crossed the bitter fault lines of white versus black; or Boer versus Brit?

I admire the leadership of the War Museum for being courageous enough to open up this site of memory for broader interpretation. The challenge for South Africa, now riding the emotional crest of a re-energised rainbow nation as a result of the wonderful Soccer World Cup event, is to take another look at our history in ways that bring about those priceless gifts of humility, acknowledgment, reparation, reconciliation, solidarity and hope.

That will depend, of course, on how we answer questions about the past. And so I ask you: how would you have answered the young boy's question?

Being respectful is a choice

Intellectuals have a responsibility not to inflame hatred

26 May 2010

Would Zapiro poke fun at the Holocaust? I do not think so, and it is a sure bet that those same voices of liberal calm and democratic reason defending the cartoonist for his calculated depiction of the prophet Mohammed would explode in convulsive anger for such insensitivity; and rightly so.

I am committed to the idea of an open society. I believe firmly that there should be no holy cows in a democracy, and that the freedom of expression should have no bounds, whether in the case of religion or in the case of catastrophes.

But I also believe in decency, tolerance and respect towards those who believe differently or those injured by calamity. I believe that in a dangerous and divided world, artists and other intellectuals have a responsibility not to inflame hatred or ride roughshod over the deeply held beliefs of others.

The man appearing as a witness at the trial of Bosnian Serb militiaman, Radovan Karadžić, in The Hague, is a Muslim. Ahmed Zulic tears open his shirt to reveal on his body a Christian cross burnt into his skin by the anti-Muslim forces serving Karadžić.

There are no words to explain this atrocity adequately, let alone capture the deep emotions of humiliation and distress the man must feel. Is this the kind of world in which cartoonists should abuse their necessary liberty in order to provoke and humiliate?

In Zapiro's mind, it is all about a little sense of humour amid the burning hatreds that threaten Christian/Jewish/Muslim relationships across the globe before, but especially in the wake of, 9/11.

I tried to make a similar point to a room full of French scholars last week. Why does your government ban the burqa, I asked? The reaction was swift. France is an open society. The closing of the woman's face goes against the deepest ideals of the republic. It is oppressive to women, and that goes against the grain of what every French citizen believes about equality, liberty and fraternity. I am conscious of the fact that this is the home of the French Revolution of 1789, and that apart from colonialism, the French contributed these wonderful ideals to political cultures around the world.

There seems to be little resistance to the banning of the burqa among leftists here in Paris. 'I would not lose sleep over the decision,' says a distinguished Parisian.

It was wonderful listening to the French position on the burqa; enlightening and frank. At one level it all made sense. I kept pushing: do you really think you can legislate the behaviour of marginal groups to fit the dominant norms of your society? And did it occur to you that judging a woman's ideological commitments by what she wears might be a mistake?

There was concession, but the historical odds were against such arguments on the soil of a nation that vigorously defends its secularity, even if it offends Muslims.

'So, what is the reaction to Zapiro?' I ask a Muslim friend in South Africa, since I am out of the country. Very bad, he says, with threats of violence everywhere. A deep groan rises within my own conscience. Why, oh why, is the reaction to Zapiro's mindless provocation the threat of violence?

Which is more harmful, a cartoonist's irresponsible behaviour in lighting a match to see whether there is petrol in the car's tank, or some angry Muslims looking for a match to blow up a car filled with petrol?

We all have our religious commitments, even the most secular among us. The Holocaust is my commitment, as is my commitment towards Islam. I will not use my pen to hurt or provoke those for whom the Holocaust is a sacred (and not only a historical) memory, nor to inflame those who believe deeply that depicting their prophet in any way is hurtful and wrong.

For many Muslims, this latest attack on their faith is not simply about depiction, though; it is read as part of a much broader attack on their sacred memory. The cartoon has broader meaning, read as an assault on their identity, their culture, their belief system and their very lives – from Palestine to Baghdad, from Kabul to Karachi.

Should Zapiro be censored for what he can draw? No. Should he have exercised restraint and demonstrated respect in the use of his pen? Yes. He had a choice.

Take care, life is full of surprises

Owning up to your prejudice

12 May 2010

It is a common grievance among the black middle classes. You sit in your office. A white person comes in looking for the boss.

Before you, the boss, can respond, the white visitor, with bobbing head, looks behind you and asks of the open air: 'Is anyone here?'

I have heard, and indeed experienced, this situation so many times that it isn't funny anymore.

So, last week, I set off to meet a brilliant young professor with a distinctively Afrikaans surname at one of our leading universities. The young woman had achieved what few scholars attain so early – a world-class research rating with impressive research publications.

She is a Botha (not her real Afrikaans-sounding name) at a formerly white university. In my mind, I held an image of a tall, white Afrikaans-speaking woman whose relative privilege must explain these scholastic achievements.

I made my way to Prof. Botha's office, knocked briefly and turned the door handle. In front of me appeared a smiling, short, black woman with my kind of hair.

My head bobbed briefly to look behind her to see whether Prof. Botha was in an office adjoining that of the secretary.

When I saw a solid wall behind the still-smiling short professor, my heart sank and I blurted out: 'I thought you were ...'

The black professor let me down gently with just a hint of criticism: 'I'm sorry to disappoint you.'

I felt thoroughly ashamed of my prejudice and I can only pray that Prof. Botha will find it possible to forgive me.

No black (or white) person I know owns up to his or her bigotry and prejudice. We eagerly point out this cancer in other people, but it is simply not a problem of ours.

And yet, not a day passes without many of us making snap judgments about our brothers and sisters based on ingrained expectations about what the other side will think or do. Our choices are more often than not racially informed, a consequence of sometimes long and bitter experience at the hands of the other side.

The men who invited me to lunch in Pretoria call themselves *Boere-veterane* (Boer veterans). They urgently wanted a meeting because, they claimed, I could help 'their people'.

Slightly nervous about accepting the invitation, my curiosity got the better of me. And so, on my next trip to Pretoria, I fitted in lunch with these men.

I had prepared my arguments about the virtues of non-racialism and the need for them to change the outdated name of their organisation and join the struggle against poverty, illiteracy and disease.

I was going to take no nonsense from this group and would treat them to a hard-hitting lecture on transformation.

That was the plan.

Around the table sat seven older, hardened men. I recognised some of them – one a prominent military leader during the apartheid years; the other a commissioner from the Truth and Reconciliation Commission.

No bother, my corrective lecture was ready for delivery.

But they spoke first.

The men told of their dedication to South Africa. They spoke with care and concern about making our country great. Despite the obvious challenges facing the nation, they want to be part of the transformation of society.

'How can we use our skills,' they asked, 'to help those who are in need?' I choked with emotion as the salad in my lower throat refused to succumb to the peristalsis of my oesophagus.

If we simply took the time to reflect on our daily experiences across the accident of skin colour, we would recognise that these experiences are not so uncommon.

In a state of racial anger and racial suspicion, we are not able to respond to, let alone appreciate, sacred moments that invite us into communion with our brothers and sisters on the other side.

La Rochelle High School in Paarl has just turned 150 years old. Last week, they invited me to speak to a diverse group of Grade 12 school leaders drawn mainly from the top rural schools in the Western Cape.

I spoke about the key leadership qualities required of leaders in a broken world. Afterwards, long lines of student leaders formed to tell me how much they had appreciated the lecture.

One white Grade 12 girl from Vredendal waited until the end and called me to one side to say the following: 'Scripture says words can mean little. Can I rather give you a hug?'

Vulgarity tip of amoral iceberg

Stripping away public decency

28 April 2010

Is it me, or are there now more people urinating along our roads than ever before? I see it in big cities and small towns, in full view of passing traffic and in shallow bushes, on major highways and in small streets, in sizes large and small, in black and white.

One fellow even waved to me the other day while occupied in the bush – a sarcastic brush-off kind of wave that meant 'look elsewhere'. Our people have descended to a level where the once-hallowed public toilet is becoming redundant. I have been thinking a lot about how South African society came to this point. What on earth is going on?

This might be a stretch for the serious social scientist, but I think there is a possible link between the ease with which citizens spray their waste matter in public spaces, the way in which protesting workers spray public waste across our streets, and the way in which public figures spray verbal waste across the airwaves. In other words, what we are seeing is a general vulgarisation of South African society, which is slowly but surely stripping away any sense of public decency on the part of ordinary citizens.

Nowhere is this image of widespread vulgarity in society more powerfully depicted than on the cover of Xolela

Mangcu's fascinating book, *The Democratic Moment: South Africa's Prospects under Jacob Zuma*. In the cover photo, a man stripped to his underpants weaves his way ahead of a protesting group, with a photo of Zuma seen ahead of him.

There are other images that come to mind, such as the pulling down of pants in public at the election of the ANC Youth League president, or the shouting down of the nation's president at a ruling party congress.

The way in which public figures deal with such vulgarity suggests that it is just going to get worse. Take the strike of the South African Municipal Workers' Union the other day. Here, these good citizens of Gauteng go on the rampage, splitting open black refuse bags and emptying garbage cans onto the streets of Johannesburg, even as they make what might well be legitimate demands for more money or improved working conditions. But they trash the city to make that point.

Then, our political and municipal leaders sit down with these vulgar people and obediently bow to their demands. After all, these images fly across a soccer world already reeling from seeing repeated images of recent high-profile murders. In part because of habit and in part because of embarrassment, our leaders bow to the demands of the vulgar.

Parents will be familiar with this kind of childish tantrum. Early in his or her life, your child will test you. You make the rule of no ice cream before dinner and the child flies into a fit. Good parents discipline that child on the spot, making it clear that the next time they even think of having a tantrum, they stand to lose a limb. Bad parents give in to the temper tantrum and the child knows that the next time she is denied ice cream, she should throw another tantrum. The logic is simple: it works.

The same is true of the way in which some university managers deal with student protests. There is a cut-off date for registration negotiated with the student representative council. The date comes. The students decide that the closing date is unnecessary and inconvenient. Yes, they do not have money and yes, they have failed a string of subjects. But they see the responsibility of university leaders as keeping the doors of learning open, whether or not they have enough money to pay their staff, and whether or not the students stay in the university system for five or ten years to obtain their degree. When they are not heard, the students decide to burn some residences, trash the library and throw rocks through windows.

I know more than one university in which the leaders sit down with the students and then change the closing date for registration. This is how universities became bankrupt in the 1990s, and how a culture of violent protest became predictable on half a dozen campuses. The vulgar nature of these protests should concern us all.

What happens, we should ask, when vulgarity (defined in my dictionary as 'conspicuously and tastelessly indecent') becomes normal in a society? That is, when being decent and respectful becomes the aberration, and vulgarity is the more common practice?

The immediate consequence is that human relationships suffer and human beings begin to turn on each other. Then, rules of common decency no longer apply, as in the case of the vulgar men who attacked a helpless baby in Randburg last week.

Sing of life, or sing of death

Untransformed race relations in rural South Africa

7 April 2010

Every now and again something happens that forces South Africa to stare its still unresolved racial troubles in the face.

So it was with the death at the weekend of Eugène Terre'Blanche – as it was with the St James Church massacre, the Skierlik shootings and the Reitz incident, to name but a few. At such points, as angry white citizens face off angry black citizens, the nation has a choice.

It can descend into a racial feeding frenzy of bitterness, accusation and retaliation. Or it can draw people together in a common cause to learn from an atrocity, and to build lasting foundations for peace and social justice.

For the latter to happen, strong leadership needs to be asserted that brings people together in dialogue and deliberation. Sadly, time after time, such leadership is in short supply.

The easy part is the shouting, the threats, the reaction to what seems obvious. 'He lived and died by the sword,' many said. 'Served him right,' I heard often. The difficult part is asking what was really going on. Let's take another look at the murder of South Africa's most emboldened white supremacist.

Few people deliberate on the still untransformed race relations that characterise the rural landscape of the country. On many farms in this land, old relations of white *baasskap* and black servitude remain unchanged, despite broader democratisation of society. This is where physical intimidation, assault or insult remain the experiences of many farm workers.

Black anger has been building up steadily. Small wonder then that people around the farm rejoiced at the murder of Terre'Blanche. It is from these rural farmlands that many white students come to university, demanding the same kinds of relationships. Placed inside the intimate confines of shared residences, trouble is unavoidable.

But take another look at the farmlands of South Africa. Now change your spectacles. On plots and smallholdings, on small and large farms, sit an increasingly scared people. They are white, and more of them are becoming poor. They have erected all kinds of barricades and organised local security teams to protect them against the invasion of farms by black criminals who maim and murder on a regular basis. The police are slow to respond; murderers are seldom caught.

Day after day, the Afrikaans dailies carry gruesome photographs and lead stories about white people, Afrikaners, murdered on their farms. Afrikaans radio stations, such as Radio Pretoria, repeat the details of these massacres over and over again.

Then, to further stress and strain the nerves of these vulnerable farmers, they hear a song with unmistakable murderous lyrics being revived from within the ruling party. It is not only that ANC Youth League leader Julius Malema leads the singing; it is also that his seniors, including the secretary-general of the Party, defend it.

Worse, the president of the country is silent on the matter. Does this mean that the killing of Boers again enjoys official sanction? No amount of reinterpreting of the song in its historical context helps those who feel the heat of exposure and attack on these farms. It is like the security forces of old trying to tell black people that to 'permanently remove from society' (as erstwhile security documents revealed) does not mean kill the activists. Kill means kill.

Then another farmer dies in his dilapidated farmhouse, his face hacked into pieces through the systematic blows of a panga and knobkerrie. A movement that was slowly dying out, the Afrikaner Weerstandsbeweging (AWB), suddenly gets three thousand new signatories, if its leaders are to be believed. Racial hatred and confrontation are back in public view.

'Should I pack my bags and leave now?' a black stranger asked me in a shop the other day.

The country will not implode. The AWB has no force any longer. The middle ground of decent white and black South Africans is too strong. But these incidents of racial attack slowly but surely erode the confidence of the economic classes that are keeping the country afloat. Without leadership that deals with underlying causes – and not only symbolic acts (important though they are), such as visiting white squatters – these incidents will recur.

What can be done?

Stop the singing of that pernicious song immediately. It is hurting all our people. Intervene in the rural farming areas, not by threatening white farmers with confiscation of their land, but by building relationships between farmers and farm workers that are dignified and respectful. This will eventually lead to a peaceful resolution of the land problem.

Incapacitated by incompetents

Political credentials trump competence

31 March 2010

How did competence become a bad word? When last did you hear a South African talk about anyone as being competent?

I have not for a long time heard that word used to describe a politician – or any public servant, for that matter. Competence is an achievement that is more likely to make you lose your job than keep it.

This is the problem of Pravin Gordhan now, as it was of Trevor Manuel then.

You do your job well, like preventing our economy from becoming a Third World basket case, and some group or other will line you up for public execution. They will not accuse you of incompetence because that is obviously not the problem; they will call you 'neoliberal' (trust me, they do not know what that word means) or 'counter-revolutionary' (although they themselves are certainly not revolutionary), but the goal is to strike down any appearance of competence at the job.

It is why Mavuso Msimang failed to transform Home Affairs – it was not simply because incompetence is deeply embedded in the organisational culture of this notorious department. It was that incompetence was protected, nourished and defended by the powerful when Msimang had the temerity to try and transform this business.

Let's be frank: too many people depend on a corrupt and inefficient Home Affairs for a newcomer to demand competence and take away a steady stream of income from the parasites inside and outside the department, who feed daily on this rotten carcass with the homely name.

My dictionary is funny. It defines competence as 'the quality of being adequately or well-qualified physically and intellectually'. Oh boy.

The mind drifts involuntarily to the police force. Did you see that video clip of the policemen, led by their commander-in-chief, chasing some criminals down a field somewhere in the beloved country? There they were, protruding stomachs bouncing along ahead of the rest of their bodies.

The question that must have crossed every thinking mind was: who will get there first, the stomach or the policeman? Don't get me wrong, I'm no Twiggy myself. But then again, I am not running (oops) after criminals.

'Well-qualified physically', my foot! We appoint policemen to the job precisely because there is no qualification required, whether physical or intellectual.

The truth is, you need not be competent to find a job in South Africa. You need the right political credentials; you need the right networks. It helps if you have the right colour – the darker the skin, the better. And it helps if you make the right noises, show up at the right funerals and embrace the right scoundrels. But whatever you do, do not

– under any circumstances – demonstrate competence; it could cost you your deployment.

We created an academic industry as progressive critics of the practice of the Afrikaner nationalists or IFP ethnicists of linking employment to ideological or tribal loyalty in the bad old days. Now we are doing the same thing, with the same results.

When last did you sit on an interview panel for a job in the new South Africa and hear someone ask the obvious question: are you competent to do the job?

You will notice that people may sneer when you arrive early for work or leave late. What is she trying to prove? Why keep serving people when they stand in a long queue in the blazing sun? It's your lunchtime, after all! Bugger the people.

When I served as dean at the University of Pretoria, most of our academics were housed in one building on the education campus.

Late at night, there would be about ten office lights burning. I discovered that the people who worked late all got their doctorates overseas. They, too, were South African, black and white, but they had learnt to labour at a different pace, to put work ahead of the timetable. They were the most productive scholars, people who hated mediocrity and were proud to be competent.

Competence does not have a colour. It is a truly non-racial attribute of the human condition.

Look carefully at the collapse of basic services in municipalities around the country. Look at the mushrooming of potholes that are sinking our provincial and local roads.

Look at how dirt stacks up, in all areas, with or without strikes. The mess is quite simply a consequence of employing (or deploying) incompetent people. When this happens, we all suffer, especially the poor.

The way forward? Make competence a respectable word once again! Be blind to politics or pigmentation when making appointments. Build capacity from the ground up, starting with the youth. Send the right signals from the top down.

Begin by firing some senior politicians for non-delivery. Then watch this country flourish.

Cast these bitter songs aside

Distinct forms of racial address plague our land

17 March 2010

The woman who has just entered the shop asks for directions to a different part of town.

She first turns to the young black woman working in the shop. Her voice is gruff, and the loudly asked question sounds like an instruction: 'WHERE is place X?'

The black woman withers, whispering that she does not know. In a huff, the inquirer turns to the older white woman behind the counter.

'Would you be so kind as to tell me where I can find place X?' Her voice is kind, gentle, almost apologetic.

The woman behind the counter does not know.

'So sorry for bothering you,' the inquirer offers.

I took in the two interactions last Saturday, wondering how often across the length and breadth of this beautiful country those two distinct forms of racial address continue to plague the land.

I am sure that if I approached the inquirer she would deny vigorously that she was a racist. She would be completely unaware of the two forms of address – one kind and gentle for the white woman; the other rough and commanding for the black woman.

The more obvious racist attacks by a white person on a black person are less evident today, compared with the years in which I was growing up. But such patterns of address, ways of talking, body language and expressions of disgust or approval continue to mark everyday interactions among South Africans.

No law can wipe out such racialised, degrading behaviours. The only way to change them is by confronting them whenever and wherever they happen. Not with a finger of accusation pointed down the throat of the offender, for that is sure to provoke outright confrontation and conflict. What disarms the offender is the soft voice of rebuke, clear and direct.

Ways of speaking can help to heal or they can provoke; they can inflame passions or settle nerves.

That is why the puzzling reappearance of the song 'Kill the Boer, Kill the Farmer' is so dangerous. It comes at a time when people's nerves are frayed because of the prevalence of vicious crime.

Like the family of the girl whose arms were severed and carried off when she was murdered in Pretoria last week.

Like the health workers who were raped when they tried to help a victim near Durban Deep.

'How are you?' I asked a group of retired South Africans over lunch the other day. 'We are murder-expectant,' they answered glumly.

There is an intellectually exciting line of research that records the ways in which teachers talk to students of different social classes (working class versus middle class), or different ethnic backgrounds. Teachers talk much more and give more instructions in classes of poor black students than in classes of upper-class white students.

That the academic results are different comes as no surprise. In schools, as in society, ways of talking are different across colour and class lines.

One day that black woman in the shop is going to explode. She will be, as they say in good English, *gatvol*. She will be out there in a service delivery protest march and she will be angry with white people passing through. All those racial slights, those gruff commands and the memories of unequal treatment will have built up inside her.

One day she will be very angry with white people and the white people will not know why.

One day, a young white boy would have heard enough from his friends, or from overhearing the grown men talk at the *braai* (barbeque). He would have heard vengeful words, stories of rape, murder and plunder against 'his people'. His peers and seniors would make it out to be a black-on-white thing.

He will pick up a gun and explode. And black people will not know why. 'He's a racist' will suffice.

Words matter. What we sing, or say in poetry or teach in classrooms can either heal or hurt. As parents, teachers, public servants or politicians we dare not leave our children without a sense of hope.

We need to nurture through words positive views of other people, especially those whom society insists are different from us.

White parents, tell your children good things about black people. Black parents, tell your children good things about white people. If you do not – and you can take my word for this – they will grow up bitter, angry, spiteful and self-destructive.

Is that what you want?

Our troubles are still skin deep

The scars of racial assault

14 October 2009

Skin is not an easy movie to watch. This brilliant retelling of the well-known story of Sandra Laing brings back powerful and painful memories. Sandra was the young girl born to white Afrikaner parents during the heyday of apartheid.

Sandra's markedly darker skin and curly hair land her in trouble at her cruel school and, before long, the tyranny of bureaucracy is intent on measuring her physical features and placing pencils in her hair in attempts to classify and reclassify the poor girl.

'Am I sick?' asks Sandra after another bout of racial prodding.

Sandra's parents fight to keep their daughter white. They work within the rules given, and insist on racial recognition according to the law. Arrangements are made to get the teenager white boyfriends, and to isolate her from interested black boyfriends.

Eventually the pressure is too much, and Sandra and her parents separate as she leaves to marry a black man. The opportunity to reconcile comes too late for her father, and to this day her white brothers refuse to meet with her.

I met Sandra Laing recently.

She is a dignified woman with enormous resilience. She is quiet spoken and reserved, without an outward trace of bitterness. But the scars of a lifetime of racial assault on her person are hard to disguise.

She is like many of my friends, who have still not met their families and who took on separate racial lives when the lighter skinned among them sought refuge and resources in the privileges afforded to skin.

Sadly, it is often the darker-skinned family members that seek out their lighter-skinned relatives.

I had a long think after the premiere of the movie at the University of the Free State this week. My black students did the predictable breast-beating to demonstrate disapproval of racism then.

One student, referring to the make-up of the audience, asked, in a question reminiscent of a recent airport incident, 'Where are the whites?'

Everybody watching the movie agreed that obsessive race thinking had demeaned people in the past.

So far, so good. Here's the problem: I don't think we have learnt from the problems of race obsession at all.

In fact, if one thing is clear to me, it is that we are doing exactly what the apartheid bureaucracy did then: treating people as if they are born into races. We still classify people into four groups.

It is black South Africans who rose up in anger at the audacity of Chinese South Africans seeking recognition as disadvantaged citizens. It is us who hunted down foreigners, separating them from authentic black South Africans.

Try and suggest another methodology for determining disadvantage – such as socio-economic status – and you will meet the wrath of black South Africa and its racial high priest, Jimmy Manyi.

So, let's not pretend that *Skin* was then, and we are now in a non-racial democracy. We still have a well-oiled bureaucratic machinery for sorting human beings by race.

It is not only tribalists who count the number of Zulus or Xhosas in the cabinet. And by insisting on something as ridiculous as 'the demographics of the country', we are doing little else than acting like our past masters.

So, where were the white students of the university?

To be frank, if I knew I was going to a film in which, once again, I would be racially accused, through the antics of my parents and grandparents' generations, I'm not sure I would show up at all.

The task of leadership is to prepare the ground for black and white students to engage with such an important film in ways that deal with our ghosts, and lay them to rest – as Mamphela Ramphele's metaphor so powerfully communicates.

But this requires the creation of a non-judgmental setting in which white students also come to confront the past. This kind of pedagogy does not exist in our schools, our universities or our society as a whole.

Maybe we are still too angry as black people. Maybe our leaders have not taught us to be generous in victory.

Maybe apartheid was just too damn successful in imprinting racial thinking deep within our consciousness.

If only we could admit that.

TALK ABOUT SPORT AND THE 2010 WORLD CUP

'No matter how successful the World Cup, South Africa sees only incompetence and demise.'

Cup brings out our true colours

There are two South Africas

30 June 2010

This Soccer World Cup has once again demonstrated that there are two South Africas.

The one South Africa is bitter, cynical, dismissive and angry. No matter what goes right in the country, it points out the wrong. No matter how successful the World Cup, it sees only incompetence and demise.

These are mainly, though not exclusively, white South Africans. They carry hurts – some of them were pained through crime and sit comfortably in Australia or other white-dominant states, but take every opportunity to rant about things down in southern Africa.

Some others cannot afford to leave and simply sit here spewing anger and filth at anything suggesting that the country is turning the corner in the economy or at Home Affairs.

Their greatest fear is that it will go well with this post-apartheid state, and that their sometimes outright racist obsessions will prove their nonsense wrong, namely that black people cannot run decent governments.

This is the South Africa of the bloggers, those faceless, idle cowards who wait up through the night for the next columnist to attack for daring to suggest that things might be going better in parts of the country. In their twisted logic, they see a seamless connection between Mugabe, Aids, climate change and teenage pregnancy.

These spoilers are also black. They are the cynical opportunists who work at Eskom, who see an opportunity to embarrass the country by launching strikes at the height of the World Cup.

They care about nothing else but their own pockets. It is a small group of people who would step on anyone to enrich themselves. They use the 'r' word recklessly ('you are a racist') to position themselves for greater advantage.

But there is another South Africa. This, I would like to believe, is the majority in the population. These are South Africans who recognise that one cannot undo 350 years of colonialism and apartheid over a weekend. They recognise our problems.

But they also acknowledge and celebrate our progress as a nation, whether it is the turnaround at SARS and Home Affairs, or the immaculate management of the World Cup. This group remains stubbornly hopeful, retaining faith in ordinary South Africans to make this country work, with or without the morally impoverished political classes.

I have heard these hundreds of voices on call-in radio stations this past week, as several hosts invited people to comment on the World Cup. The callers praised the management capacity of our leaders, the improvements in roads and transportation, the mass movement of crowds, and the efficiency of justice through the special courts.

Many of them talked about how Home Affairs had raised its game since the start of the soccer tournament. These are not mindless Pollyannas, but hopeful citizens who want us to broaden and retain the quality of these services beyond the World Cup.

I saw these people in Soweto, black and white, coming together around the two final games of the Bulls in the Super 14. I read about these people on my Facebook page, mainly students, who revel in this once-in-a-lifetime opportunity to witness the soccer extravaganza.

I observed this spirit of optimism among the thousands of volunteers giving of their time and energy.

So, with due respect to former president Thabo Mbeki, we do have two nations, but I prefer to divide our world into the cynics and the optimists; the bitter and the hopeful; the opportunists and the true patriots; the racists and the nation builders.

I got a call the day before the France versus South Africa match in Bloemfontein. It was from one of the most fearless commentators on South African public life, based in Cape Town. She said that she wanted to donate her ticket for that match to one of my students.

'But give it to the poorest of the poor!' was her instruction. I called such a student to say that the ticket would arrive by overnight courier from Cape Town. The joy of the young man was unbelievable.

The generosity of the giver was truly moving. I know of people who sacrificed their World Cup tickets and gave them to the gardener or the domestic. This is the South Africa I wish to commend today.

Into which South Africa do you fall?

Sepp says 'Collect that rubbish!'

Lessons for service delivery

23 June 2010

Why can we deliver on a multibillion rand project called the World Cup and not on simple things like collecting people's garbage on time?

There are seven reasons why we delivered on this soccer extravaganza, which carry powerful lessons for service delivery of the ordinary things frustrated citizens often complain about.

First, we delivered on the World Cup because there was single-minded leadership of this project. Day in and day out, Danny Jordaan and his senior team devoted all their energy to one single ambition: to ensure that South Africa as the host delivers on the demands that come with such a mega-event.

The leadership did nothing else; they were consumed by passion and principle not to fail. To be sure, there were the proverbial roadside bombs everywhere – like the constant media grind about crime – but the leadership of this project was focused on getting the job done, no matter what.

Second, we delivered because there were clear targets from transportation and infrastructure to media facilities and stadiums. It was clear from the outset what had to be achieved.

Once the targets were set, the plans were devised to deliver on those targets. There was no fuzzy thinking or unattainable goals. Every manager down the line knew what was expected of him or her.

Third, we delivered because there was the constant threat of withdrawal. Nothing was guaranteed.

I never believed Fifa would take the World Cup away from South Africa and give it to Australia to host; that would have been a bitter pill to swallow with our sporting nemesis down under. But the media tantalisingly reminded us of the possibility, and national pride kicked it. The message was clear: deliver or else. There is nothing like a severe penalty clause to keep service deliverers on track.

Fourth, we delivered because of the pressure of external accountability. I am open to the interesting debate on whether Fifa is simply a neo-imperialist arrangement that sucks the financial blood out of host countries, but what cannot be denied is that Fifa was to South Africa's soccer bid what good inspectors are to schools – they hold you accountable for what you have promised.

Fifth, we delivered because every citizen knew that this was not about soccer; it was about national prestige. We wanted the country to do well in the eyes of a watching world. We warmly welcomed visitors; we adorned our homes in case people needed accommodation, and we put out all kinds of literature on 'South Africanisms' to show our distinctiveness. Just imagine if every tender company delivered on its mandate by understanding the bigger picture. If every one of us who went to work every day understood that our labour was about building the nation, and not simply our own selfish demands for more material things.

Sixth, we delivered because of broad participation by all our people in this World Cup. Not a single shop did not have that string of small flags going around the perimeter of the building. Ordinary people sold everything from 'unique' South African foods to earplugs for those noisy vuvuzelas. Unemployed people with no skills were employed in their thousands in road and stadium constructions. Volunteers queued to run on and off soccer fields, whether as security guards or ball boys.

Yes, I too thought the opening ceremony was a bit bland, but what I liked was that the whole thing was organised around our people; they took centre stage in their hundreds.

Seventh, we delivered because there was the political will to do well. Did you notice that for the first time we were not subjected to that daily barrage of political parties trying to out-scream each other with the endless posturing on everything from toilets to trains?

The head of the opposition stood with the head of government, united in their determination to make the World Cup succeed from the Mother City to Soccer City. Who would have thought that in this crime-beleaguered country of ours a criminal could be arrested, convicted and dispensed to prison within the same week? Please keep those special courts that were arranged for the World Cup.

I have just returned from watching South Africa beat France at my hometown stadium here in Bloemfontein in one of the best managed public events I have ever seen.

But as I peer out of my window I see the dirt piling up because, once again, the municipality has failed to show up to collect mounds of black bags littering the street.

Even Sowetans get the Blues

Shifting political ground

3 June 2010

My friend has no sense of occasion. 'Isn't it great that all those players and fans of the Blue Bulls and Stormers descended on Soweto?' I asked.

A June 1976 activist, my now ex-friend responded glumly: 'It's true what they say; people tend to return to the scene of the crime.'

He is not alone among those refusing to buy into the emotion of this historic moment. One of the text messages doing the rounds jokes that 'the last time there were so many people wearing blue in Soweto, they were accompanied by Casspirs'. Please.

And yet there is no denying that with last Saturday's final – and the weekend before with the semi-final match of this Super 14 rugby competition – the political ground has shifted in South Africa.

Tens of thousands of white citizens came to Soweto and broke down important social, cultural and psychological barriers. For South Western Townships, or Soweto, is not only a physical place; it is also symbolic terrain. It represents political South Africa more than any other town or city.

Soweto was the site of what many believe was the turning point in the struggle against apartheid. This is home to the Mandelas, the Tutus and many other political luminaries.

Here lie the graves of struggle heroes, like Zolile Hector Pieterson, a tourist stop for those from outside the township. It was here that the white government massively miscalculated by trying to force Afrikaans onto the tongues of black people. *Taxi to Soweto*, the hilarious film, captures through humour the fears of white South Africa about black township life.

What an important moment in our democratic transition. Just a few weeks ago, there were all kinds of prophecies of a racial doomsday when the prominent white supremacist Eugène Terre'Blanche was killed by two black men.

And yet, here was the most significant non-racial celebration since that other great day when rugby broke barriers – the 1995 World Cup, when Mandela donned the white captain's No. 6 Springbok jersey.

The scene was even more impressive than in 1995. Whites were blowing vuvuzelas; here were no irritating debates about the effects of this blowpipe on white eardrums.

Breakaway shots showed Tutu eating in the stands; white clients drinking alongside black residents in local taverns (until last week they were called shebeens); whole white families being invited into black homes (*'Julle lyk honger! Kom binne'* – 'You look hungry; come inside') for the mandatory *braai*. What once was a place to fear, for many white South Africans is now a place that carries sweet memories of camaraderie and celebration across those dangerous fault lines of race.

The first time I went to Loftus Versveld, the home of the Blue Bulls in Pretoria – and where they could not play last week because of Fifa's plans for the field – a number of fans asked me to get them drinks. That was in 2002.

There were angry debates around Loftus about racial quotas in rugby; some of this noise was intended for my ears as one of the few blacks in the stands those days.

When he is drunk, you do not want to be around a male Blue Bulls fan if you're a woman or if you're black. It can get nasty.

None of this barbaric behaviour in Soweto this past month though; only joy.

On the other side of the country, a historically white political party won the election in a large black ward of Gugulethu, Cape Town.

All the theories of black political behaviour took a shot in the groin. Many black people are not that strongly wed to one party historically or emotionally, let alone epidermally; what matters more is whether you can get the job done.

What matters in rugby, as in politics, is not what colour you are, but whether you can give people a sense that they are winning.

This is the optimism I see from Cape Town to Johannesburg, as national flags suddenly sprout from the roofs of cars and drape themselves around the mirrors of vehicles.

There was no Mandela here with a green rugby top. The 'Mandelas' were not only the affable Bulls coach, Frans Ludeke, and the giant of a captain, Victor Matfield – the real 'Mandelas' were the people of Soweto, who scaled a huge emotional mountain and opened their hearts to their brothers and sisters from Pretoria. And when they did that, they found a gracious response from the other side.

It feels good to be Blue, if you know what I mean.

Why I'm no patriotic diehard

Life should not be about one place

14 April 2010

I am not proudly South African. There, I've said it; it's off my chest.

I will not wear a yellow jersey on a Friday; do not expect me to do the Diski Dance on any day, and I am no relation of Zakumi. I am not into flags, and I sing the national anthem only because everybody watches my mouth at graduation ceremonies to see whether I continue singing the Afrikaans '*Uit die blou van onse hemel*' part.

National identity was the subject of a debate at the Gordon Institute of Business in Johannesburg the other night. I formed part of a panel that included two of the smartest young minds in the country, Lindiwe Mazibuko and Xolela Mangcu. The proposition for the debate was that national identity was a dangerous thing; I spoke for the motion.

Of course, I work hard in and for the country of my birth. I care passionately about what happens to schools and universities within these geographical borders. But my life has never been about one place, and nobody's should be.

The building of strong national identities is inherently exclusive; to belong to one national grouping is to exclude another. And when the stakes are high – be it the threat of terrorism from the outside, or the threat to jobs on the inside – strong feelings of patriotism quickly degenerate into strong feelings of animosity.

I bear indelible images on my mind of Zimbabwean brothers and sisters crawling through fences on the borders with South Africa, desperate to escape tyranny and to find a job. We hunt them like rabbits and hole them up in concentration camps. We then force them back across the border in trains teeming with humankind. We attack and kill them in our townships.

This is not a South African phenomenon. Notice how quickly Americans bought into the supposed 'threats to national identity', from what they called Islamic terrorists in the wake of 9/11. This kind of language got George Bush re-elected and continues to fuel American wars in Iraq and Afghanistan – wars they cannot win. For there to be an 'us' united behind patriotic symbols, there's got to be a 'them'. And that's where the trouble starts in unequal societies.

History, of course, is on the side of such an anti-nationalist position. African borders, radical thinkers like to say, are colonial constructions. That's right. Then why would post-liberation movements defend those borders with such venom? Not too long ago, in archaeological time, our forbears crossed these imaginary borders back and forth, giving birth, marrying, fighting, building and dying on a common soil.

Watch the treatment of Mexicans streaming across the borders into the southern states of the USA and you will understand why the richest nation in the world has a

Department of 'Homeland Security'. By the logic of history, of course, the Mexicans occupied much of North America long ago. But the nationalist sentiment that fuels strong feelings of national identity does not tolerate the long view.

I teach my own children and my students to think of themselves as human beings occupying a common planet. Their pain must be borderless, and take in the trauma of a mother who lost her child to an American bomb in Afghanistan, as well as that of an American soldier who has just lost his leg to a roadside bomb.

Their values should be universal, holding up for judgment both the president of Sudan and the prime minister of Britain for going to war against other human beings.

My message is more easily understood by this first generation of 'knowledge workers', who are more likely to work in five or more countries in their lifetimes than their grandparents are. They understand that polluting a climate is a borderless threat, and that global finance is an exchange that happens in real-time at planetary speed. The old-fashioned ideas of 'proudly anything' are meaningless in an interconnected world.

Nobody who takes this line in a South African debate can ever win. For too long, essentialist thinking has been injected into our apartheid veins to force us to think of ourselves as Zulu or Afrikaner or Pedi. Too many South Africans really believe that there is such a thing, which is why my friend Ivor Chipkin's new book, *Do South Africans Exist?* will sell poorly.

Of course, I will show up at the Fifa World Cup celebrations. But not to support one team, let alone a candidate for first-round expulsion. I will show up to celebrate the greatest game ever played by human beings. And, in so doing, I hope we can bring a divided and unequal world together to celebrate our common heritage.

Jansen shoots ... he scores!

The great game

13 January 2010

It was raining heavily that morning before school started. But the game had to go ahead. There, in the off-white sands of my primary school, the student-organised finals of the interclass competition were being played with a tennis ball. Every now and again the ball would disappear under the sand.

At times the rain belted down so heavily that we took a break before restarting. This match had been planned for weeks; we sat up the weekend crafting strategy. Few had slept the night before as the excitement mounted. It was a game to be played to the death.

A penalty would seal the game. We pretended being surrounded by roaring crowds in imaginary stadiums, holding their collective breath and then sighing as the poor tennis ball soared over the school fence.

'Goal,' shouted the one team. 'Too high,' said the opposition, then provoking with sarcasm: 'but ... three points in rugby!' A scuffle broke out.

We cursed the school bell as we started classes in rain-soaked uniforms.

A few years later, some of the same boys gathered at the home of a friend to watch a grainy video of Brazil playing in one of the Soccer World Cup finals. The video was smuggled into the country, but nobody cared because more than one 'bubby' (the Indian shopkeepers) sold the contraband on the sly.

Our mouths hung open as a curler from a Brazilian forward (they all had one name, like Pele or Socrates) swung into the top of the net. We cursed apartheid before we fought it, for South Africa was banned from access to these world sports. Otherwise we would have been able to watch the match live on television or on a decent video recording.

Like so many boys in South Africa, soccer was all we did. We played before, during and after school. Under the lonely lampposts of a dimly lit street, there on the Cape Flats, we played until our parents threatened us with violent death unless we came inside immediately. You would walk towards the gate of your house, but just as you were about to go inside and obey parental orders, the ball would miraculously show up at your feet, with the opposing goalie at your mercy.

Back you went into play as a car swerved to avoid hitting you on the narrow tarred road where the game was being played.

Suddenly, I felt my body being lifted from the ground. Was this the Rapture, that event that evangelical Christians believe would lift them from the earth into the heavens at the second coming of Christ? I was soon to be relieved of this fantasy, for my upward trajectory eventually ended in a dirt bin. My normally placid and long-suffering father had had enough of my disobeying orders. The rest of the soccer team erupted in laughter, finally ending our sizzling game of soccer.

The only other time my father whacked me was in primary school. Ours was the poor man's game; all you needed was a ball. And so, during the school intervals, my blazer marked the place of an imaginary football post. When the bell rang, however, we ran for class and forgot the blazer.

This happened three times in one month. For my father, on his driver's salary, this was a devastating loss. He teared up as he reluctantly whacked my bottom.

There were not many soccer teams around in the late 1960s and early 1970s, but we all had one. Since most of my class chose Cape Town City, I chose the local opposition, Hellenic. We also had an English soccer team, mine was – and to this day remains – Tottenham Hotspur. I had stacks of cards featuring favourite players, and these were part of a burgeoning trade in cards among friends. Soccer consumed our lives.

I was never very good at any sport, but I played everything available – chess, cricket, rugby, the 800 m race – and even forced myself into the school's senior soccer team. Of all the sports, though, soccer was the great game.

It is 2010 and the boy in me cannot believe that the greatest sports extravaganza, the Soccer World Cup, is being played on our doorsteps! No more grainy videos from bubby under the sports boycott. No more imaginary soccer crowds. No more soccer magazines featuring players we would never meet.

This is it and, whether by hook or by crook, I am going to get a ticket to a game. We have waited long enough.

More good than bad in SA

We are standing and that means we have hope

16 December 2009

'This train will not go any further,' says the voice over the intercom, 'because of a person under the train.'

'This is not completely uncommon,' says my friend, with clumsy English reserve, 'especially in the holiday season.' A human being was under a train. Who knows what troubles she carried and what pain she endured to have caused this desperate act. The loss of human life brings shock, and then reflection.

This is the time of the year to reflect; to look back on one of the most dramatic years in recent South African history.

More than one media prophet expected the sky to collapse. A president was replaced or, in polite language, recalled. A world economic crisis swept through the land. Old heads tumbled, from the Ministry of Finance to the Reserve Bank to Eskom to Athletics South Africa, and new heads took their place.

The more radical face of government was supposed to send shock waves through the capitalist establishment. And yet, here we are at the end of the year, and things look more or less like they always did, despite the noise.

That our country has troubles is clear, yet we still remain a beacon of hope for so many outside South Africa who remember the great step we took away from the abyss of the late 1980s into Africa's last new democracy.

In many parts of the country things are looking up. Suddenly, we have clarity on our Aids policy, which just might begin to stem the tide of recklessness that has marked governmental leadership for the past decade.

For the first time, we have a Minister of (Basic) Education who says unequivocally that outcomes-based education is not working and that new plans are required. And the bold proposals from a major African polluter (that's us) on matters of climate change is something to be proud of.

I cannot think of a country with better beaches, more striking mountain ranges, more graceful harvest fields, or more creative energies among its peoples. This is the country to which thousands will migrate in a few months to witness the most spectacular sport on earth. They will be astounded, even mesmerised, by African culture, custom and character – and see a part of South Africa that even the natives will be moved by.

We will host visitors with pride, and for a few months all our troubles will seem distant.

It would be easy to slide into pessimism about the future, but the truth is our economy is holding on a continent with little to show in terms of economic stability; we have witnessed at least three peaceful transitions of government; our major roads are improving, thanks to a massive public works programme; and we still produce the largest numbers of foreign teachers for places such as the

United Kingdom – more than any other Commonwealth country.

I shall remain a critic of our many troubles – crime, poor schools, and poverty to begin with – but I think we should also take stock of how fortunate we are. It is easy to forget that, not too long ago, political prophets spoke of a bloodbath in our country as we entered the 1990s.

It would be a mistake to think that the deep trauma of three centuries of occupation will be easily or quickly overcome. Too much damage has been done to people and to institutions to expect an easy transition. But at least we're standing, and that means we have hope.

This country is held together by the unseen goodwill of millions of its citizens: the mother who funds the education of her domestic's child at the same school as her own daughter; the religious communities that take food to the hungry in informal settlements; the voluntary groups that take toys and clothes to abandoned children in a home so that they too have a sense of Christmas or Eid; the businessmen who raise money for university bursaries over and above the social responsibility deposits they make dutifully each year.

Whatever else we offer young people, the most important gift is hope. We must constantly convey a sense that things can be better, and boost the capacity to make a difference among those around us.

Even as we rightfully point out what is wrong in our society, we must also acknowledge what is going right. A society that sinks into chronic pessimism encourages the kind of desperation like that of the person under the train.

EPILOGUE

Reconciliation nights – the Reitz saga draws to a close

3 March 2011

The tension is unbearable. This would be the first time since 2007 that the four former students and the five workers would meet face to face, and this at the scene of the tragedy, the university campus. We all know that Thursday, 24 February 2011, will be a long night.

True to custom, the four boys – now grown men – are there on time, waiting. I study their eyes and their body language. One can feel the nervous tension emanating from their bodies with the more reserved handshake.

So far they have managed to stay out of the scrutiny of the public eye, except for the endless replays of the scenes of what appears to be a series of games played by students and workers but which turned out to be a racist attack on the black staff as a means of protesting against racial integration in the campus residences. But now, after long and complex negotiations between the three parties involved – the university, former students and staff – an agreement has been reached to settle the matter out of court.

While the former students have come alone, the five workers have brought their families. The dinner that has been arranged might or might not happen in Room 16, where family and food await the outcome of the drama down the corridor in the rector's seminar room. This seminar room has been the site of many difficult dialogues during my twenty months on the campus; it is also the room where the historic meeting between Julius Malema and myself took place late in 2009. If only the walls of that room could talk ...

There is a snag. One, and then two, of the women workers first want to meet alone with one of the boys. This is risky, because if something goes wrong, a private confrontation could demolish months of hard work by the three sides.

When we hear the request, it is clear that this is to be a serious moment. The first woman wants to meet with the boy whom she knew longest, and whom she expected to defend her dignity among the other boys. She wants to know how he could have let her down. She wants an explanation before the bigger meeting with all nine participants. I cannot imagine what pain these two engagements will bring, but I leave the small room with one of the workers crying. I call the psychologist to join them.

Then the big meeting in the seminar room. I thank the three groups for coming together of their own volition, and for recognising the limits of legal remedies for complex human problems. Should they come to an agreement, there would be one more hurdle to cross, the public apology the next evening. They should prepare emotionally and spiritually for the intense exposure to a mixed audience of sceptics and supporters, and the searching cameras and lights of local and international media.

Then it would be over, and they could get on with the rest of their lives. We agree to limit the media exposure,